Methodism: A Very Short Introduction

T0055130

VERY SHORT INTRODUCTIONS are for anyone wanting a stimulating and accessible way into a new subject. They are written by experts, and have been translated into more than 45 different languages.

The series began in 1995, and now covers a wide variety of topics in every discipline. The VSI library currently contains over 600 volumes—a Very Short Introduction to everything from Psychology and Philosophy of Science to American History and Relativity—and continues to grow in every subject area.

Very Short Introductions available now:

ABOLITIONISM Richard S. Newman
ACCOUNTING Christopher Nobes
ADAM SMITH Christopher J. Berry
ADOLESCENCE Peter K. Smith
ADVERTISING Winston Fletcher
AFRICAN AMERICAN RELIGION
   Eddie S. Glaude Jr
AFRICAN HISTORY John Parker
   and Richard Rathbone
AFRICAN POLITICS Ian Taylor
AFRICAN RELIGIONS
   Jacob K. Olupona
AGEING Nancy A. Pachana
AGNOSTICISM Robin Le Poidevin
AGRICULTURE Paul Brassley
   and Richard Soffe
ALEXANDER THE GREAT
   Hugh Bowden
ALGEBRA Peter M. Higgins
AMERICAN CULTURAL HISTORY
   Eric Avila
AMERICAN HISTORY Paul S. Boyer
AMERICAN IMMIGRATION
   David A. Gerber
AMERICAN LEGAL HISTORY
   G. Edward White
AMERICAN NAVAL HISTORY
   Craig L. Symonds
AMERICAN POLITICAL HISTORY
   Donald Critchlow
AMERICAN POLITICAL PARTIES
   AND ELECTIONS L. Sandy Maisel
AMERICAN POLITICS
   Richard M. Valelly

THE AMERICAN PRESIDENCY
   Charles O. Jones
THE AMERICAN REVOLUTION
   Robert J. Allison
AMERICAN SLAVERY
   Heather Andrea Williams
THE AMERICAN WEST Stephen Aron
AMERICAN WOMEN'S HISTORY
   Susan Ware
ANAESTHESIA Aidan O'Donnell
ANALYTIC PHILOSOPHY
   Michael Beaney
ANARCHISM Colin Ward
ANCIENT ASSYRIA Karen Radner
ANCIENT EGYPT Ian Shaw
ANCIENT EGYPTIAN ART AND
   ARCHITECTURE Christina Riggs
ANCIENT GREECE Paul Cartledge
THE ANCIENT NEAR EAST
   Amanda H. Podany
ANCIENT PHILOSOPHY Julia Annas
ANCIENT WARFARE
   Harry Sidebottom
ANGELS David Albert Jones
ANGLICANISM Mark Chapman
THE ANGLO-SAXON AGE John Blair
ANIMAL BEHAVIOUR
   Tristram D. Wyatt
THE ANIMAL KINGDOM
   Peter Holland
ANIMAL RIGHTS David DeGrazia
THE ANTARCTIC Klaus Dodds
ANTHROPOCENE Erle C. Ellis
ANTISEMITISM Steven Beller

Available soon:

For more information visit our website

www.oup.com/vsi/

William J. Abraham

METHODISM

A Very Short Introduction

OXFORD
UNIVERSITY PRESS

OXFORD
UNIVERSITY PRESS

Great Clarendon Street, Oxford, OX2 6DP,
United Kingdom

Oxford University Press is a department of the University of Oxford.
It furthers the University's objective of excellence in research, scholarship,
and education by publishing worldwide. Oxford is a registered trade mark of
Oxford University Press in the UK and in certain other countries

First edition published in 2019

Impression: 2

Published in the United States of America by Oxford University Press
198 Madison Avenue, New York, NY 10016, United States of America

British Library Cataloguing in Publication Data
Data available

Library of Congress Control Number: 2018968137

ISBN 978-0-19-880231-0

Printed in Great Britain by
Ashford Colour Press Ltd, Gosport, Hampshire

To Robin Lovin

Contents

List of illustrations

Chapter 1
John Wesley and the origins of Methodism

The numbers

Methodism was initially a movement to bring spiritual vitality to the Church of England in the 18th century. In order to do so it cultivated intimate experience of God, tangible care for the poor and needy, creative and effective forms of evangelism, a generosity of spirit to other Christians, and a clever combination of small, intimate groups and big, public gatherings. In the 19th century it became the largest Protestant denomination in the United States of America. The term 'Methodist' was initially a pejorative nickname turned into a badge of honour; it denoted the methodical way in which Methodists approached their relationship with God. In time it expanded into a network of Methodist and Wesleyan denominations across the world. Close to eighty million worldwide trace their lineage back to the Methodists of the 18th century. If we include the spiritual children and grandchildren who have arisen from groups stemming from Wesley, then we have astronomical figures, for we have to add the 250 million Pentecostals and Charismatics across the globe. Strictly speaking these groups are not Methodist, but they very clearly stem from Methodism. The crucial bridge between Methodism and these groups is the Holiness Movement in the United States that paved the way for them by insisting on a second experience of baptism in the Holy Spirit. Pentecostals and

Charismatics shifted the focus to the experience of the Holy Spirit at Pentecost in the book of Acts and sought thereafter to unpack and revise their vision of the work of the Holy Spirit in the light of the events depicted there. Hence, if we add in this network of Christians, we are looking at more than one in four Christians alive today; and more importantly we are looking at the most vibrant form of Christianity in the contemporary world. However, this wider network is beyond the scope of the current work.

An accident waiting to happen

Methodism really started as an accident; there was no intention to form a movement or a church in the mind of John Wesley, the crucial architect behind it all. Charles Wesley, his collaborating brother, was even less interested in doing anything that would involve breaking away from the mother church. They were both buried as sons of the Church of England. Their parents had originally been Dissenters; however, they had been intellectually converted to the Anglican Church while still young. They had produced a large family—nineteen children in all; with John quite possibly having been the fruit of reconciliation after a domestic row over prayers for the king. Susannah Wesley showed an independent streak in refusing to pray for the reigning monarch, William III. John was born on 17 June 1703 and lived until 2 March 1791. Charles was born on 18 December 1707, and died on 29 March 1788. Where John was clearly the intellectual and organizational genius of the movement, Charles was an extraordinary hymn-writer who summed up the heartbeat of Methodism in over 6,000 hymns and poems.

Early life of John Wesley

John Wesley's spiritual journey became in time a model for many who went on to become his followers. He began as a faithful son of Anglicanism, initiated into its theology and piety at Charterhouse School and Oxford University. His spiritual life took off when he began to immerse himself in books on holiness that fired his imagination. The quest for holiness, known almost universally in his day as a quest for Christian perfection, remained absolutely central to his work and mission. After completing his degree he became a Fellow of Lincoln College, happy to take on the life of a teacher in the university. Had he stayed the course, he would have become an outstanding theologian. He certainly had the training and gifts to do so. However, his life was redirected in a series of developments in the 1730s that culminated in his becoming an extraordinary evangelist and spiritual director.

He was ordained first as a deacon and then as a priest. He joined a band of young people led by his brother who were deadly serious about their spiritual lives and who met for study, prayer, sacramental practice, and outreach to the local prison in Oxford. The group was given various nicknames: Bible Christians, Bible Moths, and Methodists. Wesley picked up the last and used it as a badge of honour. It started off as a term of ridicule, applied well beyond the Wesleyan group, but it was eventually restricted to apply only to those who became his followers. He was subsequently recruited with Charles to go to Georgia as a missionary. In this endeavour he was essentially a total failure, expecting the locals there to adopt the regimen of discipline established at Oxford. After an aborted love affair, he was put on trial and high-tailed it out of town before a verdict was reached. However, in the course of his travels he was confronted by a piety among German missionaries known as Moravians that shattered his confidence and forced him to take a deeper look at his relationship with God. He was amazed at the courage the Moravians showed in the face of impending death on the high seas; he was equally confounded by the theology their leaders taught. They insisted on a level of assurance and victory over evil that tempted him to question radically his own spiritual condition. In typical fashion, he set about examining their claims as if a lawyer consulting his law books and cross-examining the best witnesses he could find.

The Aldersgate experience

In a meeting in Aldersgate Street on 24 May 1738, after a visit to St Paul's cathedral, John found himself overwhelmed by the reality of God and divine grace. He described it in the following fashion.

> In the evening I went very unwillingly to a society in Aldersgate Street, where one was reading Luther's preface to the Epistle to the Romans. About a quarter before nine, while he was describing the change which God works in the heart through faith in Christ, I felt my heart strangely warmed. I felt I did trust in Christ, Christ alone for salvation: And an assurance was given me, that he had taken away my sins, even mine, and saved me from the law of sin and death.

His brother Charles reported a similar experience three days earlier on the Feast of Pentecost, 21 May 1738. Charles had come to see himself as living in a 'legal night' that left him without assurance. Earlier, he too had been challenged by the same Moravian leader, Peter Böhler, who had confronted John about his spiritual condition.

> 'Do you hope to be saved?' [asked Böhler] 'Yes,' I replied. 'For what reason do you hope it?' 'Because I have used my best endeavors to serve God'. He shook his head and said no more. I thought him very uncharitable and said in my heart: 'What, are not my endeavors a sufficient ground of hope? Would he rob me of my endeavors? I have nothing else to trust to.'

Some time later, having fallen ill, Charles was staying with a friend, John Bray, who shared with him Luther's commentary on Galatians. Luther brought him face to face with the doctrine of justification by grace through faith. This intellectual confrontation changed his life.

> At eight I prayed for myself for love; with some feeling, and assurance of feeling more. Towards ten, my brother was brought

in triumph by a troop of friends and declared, 'I believe.' We sang the hymn with great joy, and parted with prayer. At midnight I gave myself up to Christ; assured I was safe, sleeping or waking. Had continual experience of His power to overrule all temptation; and confessed with joy and surprise, that He was able to do exceeding abundantly for me, above what I can ask or think.

Charles had already just written the hymn that captured their new found faith.

> Where shall my wondering soul begin?
> How shall I all to heaven aspire?
> A slave redeemed from death and sin,
> A brand plucked from eternal fire,
> How shall I equal triumphs raise,
> Or sing my great Deliverer's praise?

The sixth verse captures the evangelistic impulse that the experience evoked:

> Come, O my guilty brethren, come,
> Groaning beneath your load of sin,
> His bleeding heart shall make you room,
> His open side shall take you in;
> He calls you now, invites you home;
> Come, O my guilty brethren, come!

Clearly Charles Wesley had entered a whole new phase of his spiritual journey. Two days later at the same home of John Bray, he and John joined with friends to sing the whole of this hymn with gusto. They had entered into a whole new phase of their spiritual pilgrimage and of their vocation as missionaries.

Prior to this encounter, John Wesley had been forced to rethink his understanding of God's action in Christian initiation. He was convinced that God had given him new life in baptism; however, he had sinned away the effects of that in childhood and beyond. He then became intoxicated by the quest for holiness, yet his failures in this department were all too real and he had no real assurance of God's commitment to his welfare. He also believed that, while divine grace was nominally identified as free, one somehow had to make oneself worthy of it by works of piety and mercy. This confusing vision was shattered by his rediscovery of a more radical doctrine of justification by grace through faith. This faith was a gift of God; and the Moravians taught him it was received in an instant and accompanied by immediate assurance and victory over evil. This complex of ideas played into his interpretation of what happened at Aldersgate. It is too easy to say he was born again for he already was a Christian; in reality it took him years to sort it all out. What he gained in this encounter after several months of wobbly reflection was deep personal assurance of the love and mercy of God. Even though he had been a Christian from childhood with signs to prove it, he had a whole new sense of freedom and excitement about the life of faith. So too did his brother Charles who immediately captured it in his hymns of the period.

Out in the open air

As had happened in the experience of his brother Charles, one effect of this new experience was a desire to share what he had discovered with others. Yet John was at a loss as to what to do. He conducted a study tour of the Moravian settlements on the Continent, carefully observing their well-regulated doctrines and practices. He consulted with friends from his Oxford days. One of these, George Whitefield, had also been awakened to the reality of God and had taken the bold step of preaching in the open air to thousands. In this he picked up an experiment already underway in Wales. Called away from Bristol to Wales in March of 1739, he asked Wesley to fill in. After casting lots, Wesley reluctantly launched forth. On Monday, 2 April:

> At four in the afternoon, I submitted to be more vile, and proclaimed in the highways the glad tidings of salvation, speaking

from a little eminence in a ground adjoining to the city, to about three thousand people. The scripture on which I spoke was this, (is it possible any one should be ignorant, that it is fulfilled in every true Minister of Christ?) 'The Spirit of the Lord is upon me, because he hath anointed me to preach the Gospel to the poor. He hath sent me to heal the broken-hearted; to preach deliverance to the captives, and recovery of sight to the blind: To set at liberty them that are bruised, to proclaim the acceptable year of the Lord.'

The effect was revolutionary: Wesley was confirmed in his convictions of the immediate actions of God on the occasion of preaching; and he had found a way to share that good news with others. He had found his vocation. In time he abandoned his dreams of being a scholar at Oxford, a decision heartily welcomed by university officials.

The statistics are staggering. Wesley rode up to 20,000 miles a year on horseback. He preached 800 sermons a year to crowds as large as 20,000. In a typical day he was up at 4.00 a.m.; he preached at 5.00 a.m.; and he was on the road to the next assignment at 6.00 a.m. Consider this neat snapshot of his work taken late in his life from Wednesday, 21 July 1779.

The House was filled at five, and we had another solemn opportunity. About eight, calling at Hinckley, I was desired to preach: also at Forcell, ten or twelve miles further. When I came to Coventry, I had found notice had been given for my preaching in the park but the heavy rain prevented. I sent to the Mayor, desiring the use of the Townhall. He refused; but the same day gave the use of it to a dancing-master. I then went to the women's market. Many soon gathered together, and listened with all seriousness. I preached there again in the morning, Thursday, 22, and again in the evening. Then I took the coach to London. I was nobly attended; behind the coach were ten convicted felons, loudly blaspheming and rattling their chains; by my side sat a man with a loaded blunderbuss, and another upon the coach.

Preaching in the open air was the first of a series of innovations for Wesley. One of these was to gather new converts into small groups that would enable them to survive in a hostile world. Another was the recruiting of lay preachers who would then meet in annual conferences to discuss what to do and what to teach in the societies that were formed. Later in the United States, because of exponential growth, Methodists invented General Conferences which met every four years to make decisions on matters of doctrine, church governance, mission, and the like. In time women too would be allowed to lead and preach, although this was far from easy to introduce. Yet another original experiment was to pray openly in public without a script. Such innovations, along with the claims to direct encounter with God, were challenged from high up to low down. His novelties sailed close to the limits of laws which had been set up to avoid the kind of turmoil that had torn the nation apart during the Civil War in the previous century. In response Wesley developed a small publishing industry that explained his doctrines and practices, hit back hard but cleanly against his critics, and made available a raft of sermons that summed up the heart of his teaching. He published a series of *Appeals to Men of Reason and Religion* in 1742 and 1743 that argued that he was not out of line with the tradition or with reason properly understood. Together with *The Principles of a Methodist Further Explained* (1745) and *A Plain Account of People Called Methodists* (1748) and various *Sermons*, these furnished the new movement with the theological concepts and background assumptions that were essential for long-term success.

The opposition at times was dangerous. Clergy readily organized mobs to attack him and his colleagues. In an exchange with Bishop Joseph Butler of Bristol, who called him to account for his preaching outside the boundaries of parish life, Wesley explained his rationale.

> Suffer me now to tell you my principles in this matter. I look upon all the world as my parish; thus far, I mean, that in whatever part of

it I am, I judge it meet, right and my bounden duty to declare, unto all that are willing to hear the glad tidings of salvation. This is the work which I know God had called me to; and sure I am that His blessing attends it. Great encouragement have I, therefore, to be fulfilling the work He hath given me to do. His servant I am; and, as such, am employed according to the plain direction of His word—'as I have opportunity, doing good unto all men'. And his providence clearly concurs with His word, which has disengaged me from all things else, that I might singly attend on this very thing, 'and go about doing good'.

What was at issue here was the spiritual welfare of those who preferred the ale-house to church on Sundays. Wesley was determined not just to go to those who needed his ministry but to those who needed his ministry most. He was forthright in noting the hardships involved:

> Can you bear the summer heat to beat upon your naked head? Can you suffer the wintry rain or wind, from whatever quarter it blows? Are you able to stand in the open air without any covering or defence when God castest abroad his snow like wool, or scattereth his hoar-frost like ashes? And yet these are some of the smallest inconveniences which accompany field-preaching. Far above all these, are the contradiction of sinners, the scoffs both of the great vulgar and the small; contempt and reproach of every kind; often more than verbal affronts, stupid, brutal violence, sometimes to the hazard of health or limbs or life.

Preaching in the open air was pivotal in the spread of Methodism (Figure 1). Equally important was the follow-up that gathered those interested in coming to know and love God into small groups and the organization of a band of workers who carried out Wesley's instructions on the ground. Intense piety needs intense forms of discipline for both members and workers; Wesley provided both without apology. Any renewal movement needs small groups and large meetings; again Wesley met the need.

1. John Wesley preaching in the open air.

It also requires constant review of its aims, the ability to deal with dissent from within, the provision of ideological materials, and readiness to make practical adjustments on the hoof. Over the years from the beginnings in the late 1730s, Wesley operated as a benevolent dictator who led the way in terms of personal sacrifice. He was a hopeless workaholic.

The goal of Methodism

By the early 1750s Methodism had become an evangelical order within the Church of England. When, at one of the Methodist Conferences, the question was asked, 'What may we reasonably believe to be God's design in raising up the Preachers called Methodist?', the answer given was: 'To reform the nation, especially the church, and to spread scriptural holiness over the land.' This agenda clearly required quashing the impulse to separate from the parent body, a matter taken up in 1758 with the publication of *Reasons Against Separation From the Church of England*. It also required public expression of the relevant agenda. This had already been done after a brief brush with death led Wesley in 1755 to publish his *Explanatory Notes on the New Testament*, a small volume that became, with his *Standard Sermons*, his designated account of the essentials of true religion. By 1760, the fourth volume of his *Standard Sermons* was available; to this day these are crucial for understanding Wesley's theology and are canonical for many Methodist denominations. For those who wanted to dig deeper into the history of Christian spirituality, between 1749 and 1755 he had published *A Christian Library: Extracts and Abridgements* in fifty volumes. Travelling time on horseback was not wasted; Wesley would slacken the reins and read. This led one writer two centuries later to joke that his was the kind of theology you could work out on horseback.

Wesley's endeavours were not helped by domestic developments in this period. He was attracted to a young widow, Grace Murray, who was a splendid co-worker, but he dithered, as he had earlier in Georgia with a young woman called Sophia Hopkey. Charles, who was worried about the prospects of John's marrying beneath his social class, stepped in and had Grace Murray married off to a friend, John Bennett. John Wesley was half an hour late for the marriage ceremony. He recovered by preaching, blaming God indirectly for his troubles. On the rebound he made a disastrous choice of wife in Mrs Molly Vaseille, a 41-year-old widow with French Huguenot connections. As a result he had to resign his Fellowship at Oxford. The marriage was a disaster, not least because Wesley had no intention of changing his schedule or his work habits.

Severe challenges

The 1760s produced its own crop of challenges. Thomas Maxwell, one of his first lay preachers, took the doctrine of Christian perfection to a new level, claiming to know the date of the end of the world. Wesley made clear efforts to distance himself from this kind of fanaticism. A sudden increase in membership created a serious shortage of priests to administer the Lord's Supper; Wesley sought the help of a wandering Eastern Orthodox, Bishop Erasmus, to obtain episcopal ordinations; however, the result was consternation within the ranks of Methodist leadership and not a little public embarrassment. In order to provide more cohesion across the revival, Wesley sought a plan of union with other like-minded Anglican clergy. He got nowhere with them in that they disliked his societies within their parishes and distrusted his theology. Even so, Wesley published his *Plain Account of Christian Perfection* in 1766 to rebut charges of inconsistency and theological error.

When George Whitefield, mentioned earlier, died on 30 September 1770, the theological truce that had held between Wesley and the Calvinists of the day ended. Whitefield had held that God arbitrarily chose some for heaven and damned others to hell—an ardent Calvinist, his views on predestination were detested by Wesley. Wesley found himself drawn into a nasty war with tough-minded theological opponents that lasted most of the next decade. The issues were complex on both sides. Wesley could never accept that God had drawn up a list of those destined for salvation and another of those destined for damnation. It was for him a monstrous idea that threatened the universal love of God, undermined the quest for holiness, and undercut his work in evangelism intended to reached out to everyone. In 1778, he launched *The Arminian Magazine* to uphold his end of the debate.

Crossing the Atlantic

In the meantime, Methodism had been taken to the New World by two networks of Irish Methodists, one in Frederick, Maryland, and the other in New York. Two volunteers had gone there in 1769; and Francis Asbury, the future leader, sailed there in 1771.

The first Methodist conference was held in Philadelphia on 14–16 July 1773 and four years later the Declaration of Independence took place on 4 July 1776. When the Anglican clergy fled for their lives, Methodists were deprived of the sacraments. Wesley sought help from the Bishop of London to ordain some of his helpers. He noted that the bishop 'did see good to ordain, and send into America, other persons, who knew something of Greek and Latin; but who knew no more of saving souls, than of catching whales.' It took him years to sort out and decide what to do.

By the year 1784, Wesley decided to take drastic action, ordaining clergy for the work in North America, knowing the opposition this would elicit from his brother Charles as a loyal member of the Church of England. The American Methodists were now at liberty to follow scripture and Christian tradition and forge their own identity for a future cut loose from his apron strings. Francis Asbury was more than ready to seize the moment. Asbury was ordained deacon, presbyter, and bishop in a matter of days; a whole new and vibrant form of Methodism had been created. Deacons acted as official servants in a local church; presbyters took care of local churches; and bishops took responsibility for the general life and work of the church. Wesley had sent over a revised version of the *Book of Common Prayer* and a revised set of theological articles derived from the Church of England. These articles were simply lists of teachings, say, about the Trinity or the sacraments, officially adopted by the new church. They became the canonical doctrines of the Methodist Episcopal Church. The former was honoured more in the breach than in its usage. A new Christian denomination had been invented. The Methodists in North America were 'at full liberty to follow the Scriptures, and the Primitive Church'.

On the home front

On the home front Wesley moved to provide institutions and practices to preserve the riches of Methodism within the Church of England. He was effectively irreplaceable as a father in God to his people and as a leader of uncommon genius in terms of self-discipline, with the ability to inspire others and the skill in organizing those who came to him for spiritual help. He enacted in law a 'Deed of Declaration' that made the Conference a legal body; and he created 'The Legal Hundred' preachers as the supreme legislative body that would rule once he was gone. Even then he soldiered on, happy to preach to the end of his life. His wife, who had effectively left him in the 1760s, died in 1781. He heard too late to attend the funeral. His brother Charles died in 1788. He missed that funeral as well and broke down in public, singing one of Charles's hymns in a meeting. He founded the Strangers Friends Society in 1786 and in 1791 he wrote a letter to William Wilberforce pressing the case for the ending of slavery. In 1786, he endorsed a plan for missionary work abroad, and in 1786 he welcomed Sarah Mallet into the connection as a preacher; she was the first officially sanctioned female preacher of Methodism. Prior to this women had worked as exhorters and as extremely effective leaders of small groups.

John Wesley died on 2 March 1792. He was buried in City Road Chapel, London, one of the three geographical centres with Bristol and Newcastle. By this time he was a revered figure in the land—despite the deep misgivings about his teachings and his work as the critical founder of the people called Methodists. There is a splendid portrait of him written by a visiting scholar from the University of Uppsala in Sweden. It was written in 1769 when he was at the height of his powers:

> Today I learned for the first time to know Mr. John Wesley, so well known here in England, and called the spiritual Father of the so-called Methodists. He arrived home from his summer journey to Ireland, where he visited his people. He preached today at the forenoon service in the Methodist Chapel in Spitalfields for an audience of more than 4,000 people. His text was Luke 1: 68. The sermon was short but eminently evangelical. He has not great

oratorical gifts, no outward appearance, but he speaks clear and pleasant. After the Holy Communion, which in all English Churches is held with closed doors at the end of the preaching service, when none but the Communicants are usually present, and which here was celebrated very orderly and pathetic, I went forward to shake hands with Mr. Wesley, who already…knew my name, and was received by him in his usual amiable and friendly way. He is a small, thin old man, with his own and long and strait hair, and looks as the worst country curate in Sweden, but has learning as a Bishop and zeal for the glory of God which is quite extraordinary. His talk is very agreeable, and his mild face and pious manner secure him the love of all rightminded men. He is the personification of piety, and he seems to me as a living representation of the loving Apostle John. The old man Wesley is already 66 years, but very lively and exceedingly industrious.

It is impossible to think of Methodism in its origins as anything other than the creation of John Wesley. To be sure, lots of other folk were involved in the leadership of the movement, not least his brother Charles. However, the towering figure at its source is John Wesley, perhaps one of the least likely of candidates to be the founding father of a movement that would be international in scope and spanning centuries. He was a born leader, an independent thinker, a ceaseless workaholic, an English patriot, a conservative in politics, and a traditionalist theologian at heart. He was also a restless pragmatist, a voracious reader, a penetrating writer, a reluctant rebel, and a person full of genuine compassion for those who were towards the bottom of the social order. He was a dictator in his own Methodist household, yet he wanted to be friend of all and enemy of none. Totally devoted to divine revelation as providing the source of all his theological claims, he still sought confirmation in reason and experience for what he believed. He readily broke with tradition but not without thinking things through beforehand and not without providing a roster of reasons to defend himself. Through all his trials and tribulations he never lost faith in providence, for he believed that

God worked through everything to bring about good. He was a man intoxicated by his love of God, inexorably driven by a desire to see ordinary people become self-assured children of God, he reached out for nothing less than the perfection visible in Christ, the Son of God. In his own oddball way he was a saint who pondered long and hard about the demands and promises of God's grace amidst the rough and tumble of everyday life.

Chapter 2
Supporting background stimuli

The Moravian influence

The life of John Wesley cannot be taken in isolation. A host of factors, personal and social, were at play. His connections with the Moravians who had such a dramatic impact upon him when he was a young missionary reveal that he was part of an international network of revival and awakening that stretched from Germany to England and into the New World. On this front he is rightly seen as committed to a vision of Christianity that locates the heart of Christianity in the transformation of the human person. Call it the religion of the heart; call it the quest for holiness; call it the tradition of pietism—all of these indicate what is at issue. There is a shift from Christianity as representing a mere system of orthodox beliefs, to Christianity as a living relationship with God, leading to love of both God and neighbour. Much had been made of strict adherence to doctrine after the Reformation and the wars of religion; in many ways folk were exhausted by rival intellectual schemes of doctrine. So there was a need for fresh life to be breathed into the heart of the individual and church. The great themes of this form of Christianity are new birth—the possibility of starting all over again—and sanctification, that awkward term for genuine victory over evil, here and now.

There are dangers in this tradition; Wesley was well aware of them. He was an enthusiastic teacher in person and in print; and he was a strict disciplinarian when folk went off the rails. While something of a fanatical moralist in his judgements, he insisted that the root of moral change and enthusiasm had to be through a new life breathed into the soul by the Spirit of God. Theologically and spiritually he was a revolutionary conservative. He wanted a revival of Primitive Christianity that would change the world with the same ardour as Marxists would later long for a revolution to usher in their utopia. In all of this, he and his Methodist followers were enmeshed in a wider revitalization of Christianity in Europe and North America, with its own unique virtues and vices.

Differences with Evangelical Anglicans

John Wesley was also enmeshed in a wider network of Evangelical Anglicans who longed for reform and renewal within the Church of England. The network was made up essentially of Anglican clergy who were devoted to the renewal of their local parishes according to the ideals of the Anglican tradition. For them this meant insisting on the necessity of new birth within the ordered life of the sacraments. It also meant the rejection of innovations that would get them in trouble with the law or with the authority of their bishops. Small groups in any local parish had to be carefully monitored and kept strictly under the leadership of the clergy. Most if not all of these Evangelicals were moderate Calvinists in theology. While they avoided the extreme of believing that God had damned a select group forever and for his glory, they held firmly to the idea that human beings were much too corrupt to save themselves. Thus, they believed that salvation depended crucially on individuals being predestined to salvation entirely as a matter of divine decree and divine grace. They were also adamant about upholding the liturgical and canonical practices of the church; and they stood by the sacraments, the use of the Prayer Book, and the standard ordering of ministry. Overall, while they may have lamented the faults of their beloved Anglican tradition, they were convinced that it provided the way to spiritual renewal.

While Wesley was intimately connected with some of these Evangelical Anglicans, he really stood apart from them on several fronts. For one thing he came from a very different wing of the Anglican tradition: the High-Church tradition of his day, not to be confused with the later version of the tradition with the same name forged in the following century by John Keble, John Henry Newman, and his colleagues in the 1830s. The earlier tradition to which Wesley belonged held to a high view of the sacraments, expecting God to work objectively through them. It also held to the historic episcopate: insisting that the line of the Anglican bishops could be traced back, via the physical laying on of hands, to the apostles, thus transmitting special grace through the latter. This tradition gave the church of the first three centuries a privileged position in representing true Christianity. It was held in suspicion by those in political power for its tendency to question, for this reason, the legitimacy of reigning monarchs. This High-Church was also opposed to the distinctive doctrines of Calvin with respect to predestination. Calvin held that God simply chose certain individuals to be saved and others to be damned forever, leaving human salvation entirely to divine determinism with no relation to their individual actions.

Thus, Wesley came from a very different branch of the church than that represented by Evangelical Anglicans. After his Aldersgate experience and after he came to reject the historic episcopate, he found himself drawn to those who shared his interests in spiritual awakening throughout the land. He would dearly have loved a united front to deal with the challenges they all faced. However, his distinctive theological roots and his readiness to innovate within the structures of the Anglican tradition were too much for his potential colleagues to bear. They disliked his readiness to form Methodist societies in their parishes, maintaining his and his lay leaders' control rather than deferring to that of the local parish priests. They did not really trust him. Wesley was sailing too close to breaking the law; he evoked memories of earlier periods of civil disorder rooted in hot forms of spiritual revival. So the Evangelical Anglicans kept their distance; and eventually Wesley went his own way.

Like many of the Evangelical Anglicans who were prepared despite their differences to look upon Wesley as a friend, Wesley lamented the vices and failings of the Church of England. At times he was scathing in his evaluation of the universities, bishops, local priests, and everyday church members. This is to be expected from reformers and renewalists: they do paint in the worst possible colours in order to motivate change. It is also the besetting temptation of all moralists; and Wesley was certainly a stout-hearted moralist intent on fixing the world as fast as possible. Even so, his debt to the Church of England of his day was incalculable. As others have wisely noted elsewhere, the best traditions produce the best rebels. Wesley could not have been the person and leader he was, he could never have been the evangelist and spiritual director he was, without having access to the rich resources available to him as an Anglican.

Background stimuli

The bigger picture here is this: aside from there being a large number of folk outside the Anglican fold providing space for him to manoeuvre, Wesley was extremely fortunate in that he lived in a world where there were significant background stimuli supporting his work as a leader of a renewal movement. First, crucial features of church life helped above and beyond the theological and spiritual resources he inherited; it provided, for example, a strong tradition of sacramental practice and clear-headed preaching. Second, Wesley was aided and abetted in his endeavours by a strong evangelical movement both inside and outside the Anglican Church; he had allies who provided collateral support in the country at large. Third, he benefited from the requirements for work in and attendance at the universities that mattered: he had received a solid education that enabled him to write and argue with vigour and clarity. Fourth, he came on the scene just after others had successfully defended the core of Christian teaching intellectually; he could, as we shall see, take the general thrust of Christian belief as being already broadly culturally acceptable. Fifth, he inherited a political set up that favoured his efforts: the state endorsed and protected the Christian faith in the public arena.

Take the fact that the Anglican Church had clear doctrinal boundaries represented by the Thirty-Nine Articles (the official teachings of the Church of England), *Book of Common Prayer*, and *Homilies*. The *Homilies* were a set of sermons that could be used should the preacher fail to arrive for a service. Wesley's own canonical sermons were built around this model. These sermons together with the *Book of Common Prayer* and the Articles of Religion summarized the intellectual content of the Anglican tradition. They blended together theological material from the first four centuries with the new insights of the Reformation to provide a strong foundation of orthodox teaching. Indeed the Articles insisted on adherence to the major Creeds of the Ancient Church. All clergy were required to subscribe to the Articles of Religion. To be sure, there may have been many who merely paid lip-service to these materials. Lay members of the church did not have to agree to them; but they were constantly reiterated in worship and in a host of other ways. Thus there were excellent commentaries on the Articles available for study. The *Book of Common Prayer* was a masterpiece of English prose. The great Creeds of the Ancient Church were recited in worship. Wesley knew all of this material well enough to draw on it for his Methodist project in North America; they were also officially endorsed to be the core of Anglican sensibility.

Furthermore the universities of Oxford and Cambridge required subscription to Anglican teaching. In the century after Wesley,

John Henry Newman was put on trial in the 1830s at Oxford not on the grounds that he rejected the Articles but on the grounds that he had not subscribed to their proper interpretation. He was acquitted on a technicality but the message was clear: to teach at Oxford one had to be a loyal Anglican. Later folk would have to resign from the university because they could not subscribe. Eventually the requirement was dropped. Even so, up until the 1930s students had to take an examination in Holy Scripture at Oxford. By that time it had become something of a joke. So Wesley lived in a world where Oxford and Cambridge were faith-based universities. Again, we can be sure that many simply accepted these restrictions in a nominal fashion and otherwise thought for themselves. However, the official teachings were clear and were put forth in worship and teaching.

These official teachings had also been defended at the highest level of intellectual culture. In the 17th century, there had been significant opposition to the content of the Christian faith. The deep worry was not about belief in a generic theism, rather it was focused on the internal content of the Christian faith represented by the doctrines of the Incarnation and the Trinity. Many intellectuals were acutely challenged by the concepts of incarnation, speaking as it did of the divine becoming human in Jesus of Nazareth, and of the Trinity, with God being three persons in one substance; these concepts stretched the mind to its limits and struck many as simply incoherent. In Wesley's day, David Hume would take the debate to a deeper level and raise fundamental questions about the rationality of belief in God and belief in miracles. However, Hume kept this sceptical work under lock and key; he was content to be known at the time simply as a historian and man of letters. The crucial argument against Christianity was that it required one to accept insoluble mysteries, whereas a more generic form of theism known as deism seemed so much more rational; deists held that God was essentially an almighty, benevolent agent who created the world so efficiently that it could now function independently, without divine intervention. One could give good arguments promoting the existence of a Creator but not so easily for the Trinity. Indeed, the Christian doctrines related to salvation were morally unacceptable because they were based on special divine revelation. Such special revelation would be limited to the few; hence the doctrines derived from it could not be morally required for salvation. Figures as famous as Isaac Newton found these arguments compelling; and the great philosopher John Locke seemed to take a similar view, even though a close reading of his works would prove otherwise.

However, despite the initial attraction of generic forms of theism, there was significant push-back at the highest intellectual levels. The most compelling counter-argument was deployed by Bishop Butler, one of Wesley's opponents, in his book, *The Analogy of Religion*, which became required university reading for generations. Butler conceded that the appeal to special revelation did indeed include mysteries. However, there were also serious difficulties and mysteries related to any kind of generic theism. The problems in accepting special revelation were no more acute than those that faced a person who believed in a Creator. The critic of Christianity could either move forward and accept the whole Christian package or take a more radical position and reject theism.

This was playing with fire, for those who might accept the second option might then opt for atheism. However, for most folk this was not an attractive option; they were persuaded by the softer arguments of Butler who insisted on the importance of judgement in making theological decisions at this level. Butler was but one of a network of scholars who defended the faith of the church. In effect, they won the day in the public arena. This development was crucial for Wesley in that he could rely on their success in his own efforts to move ordinary folk into the deeper content of the Christian faith that presupposed the great doctrines of the ancient Christian tradition.

A similar effect was at work in political arrangements related to elections and leadership in government. Put simply, if one rejected, say, the doctrine of the Trinity, the game was over as far as political ambition was concerned. There was no freedom of religion as we commonly know it today. The state was a confessional state; it was faith-based in the sense that there were theological tests of membership and leadership. The Act of Toleration certainly allowed for dissent; there was no coercion as far as belief was concerned. However, dissenters were kept securely in their place outside establishment politics; they were allowed to exist and teach but they could not hold public office. The upside of this for Wesley was that he was entirely happy with the political arrangements in which the monarchy, the church, and parliament operated as a symphony, articulating and protecting the teachings and practices of the Christian faith. Taken with the factors at play within the church, within the universities, and within his intellectual world, he had significant tail-winds to speed him on his way.

As already noted, Wesley failed to recognize the favourable conditions under which he operated. He had such high standards as to what would count as a Christian nation and politics that he could only see how grim things were. There was truth, of course, in what he saw. He knew England as it was on the ground; given his travel schedule, he probably knew it better than most observers in his day. He was all too aware of the gap between official profession of faith and its actual application. He saw the effects of society's move towards industrial innovation. He knew first-hand the reality of smuggling, the grinding conditions of the poor, the hypocrisy and high-living of the upper classes, the vulgarity and violence of mobs, and the enduring struggles of everyday people. He did not have the resources of social analysis to provide much by way of causal diagnosis. He was an observer so full of curiosity and so equipped with common sense that he was not impressed by outward profession; he wanted to see inward as well as outward religion flourish. While he had a generally optimistic view of the country's political arrangements, believing that they were much better than the competing alternatives, he was also aware that the state could readily use the law against him by shutting down his operations. On the whole, he believed that the church had failed in its mission to the nation. As already noted, his job as leader of the Methodists was to reform the nation, especially the church, and to spread scriptural holiness throughout the land.

A new configuration of Christianity

It was this agenda of reform and spiritual renewal that really captured Wesley's imagination and his pragmatic instincts. The cultural platform took care of the standard teachings and practices of the church; he did not need to reinvent the wheel. He focused on what it was to become an informed and confident Christian, what it was to be a real as opposed to nominal Christian, and how to remain a Christian in what he saw as a hostile world. The task was to take faith as it had been delivered in the best form of Christianity he knew—the Anglican tradition—and have it inscribed on the hearts of the people. The crucial challenge was to see it birthed and then expressed within the church and the public order. In order to do this he ransacked the history of piety, consulted the experience of the saints in search of confirmation, had holy conversations with his assistants, and kept a steady eye on what he saw for himself among those who were his followers. Above all he immersed himself in scripture, the oracles of God that were the touchstone of truth in matters of faith and morality.

The result was a fresh if not wholly new configuration of the Christian faith. He was naïve about what could be achieved in the England of his day. Life in the rough and tumble of the inner cities would not be put right by a mere religious revival (Figure 2). He was equally naïve about what could happen by way of change in the Church of England. He never wanted his Methodist followers

2. Gin Lane by Hogarth, 1751.

to leave the church. On the one hand, the church could not
contain what he invented; it was much too radical and innovative
even though it claimed an ancient and conservative pedigree.
If he had been a Roman Catholic the powers that be might have
set him free to form an order of his own—but he was not a Roman
Catholic. On the other hand, his teachings and practices were
bound to stretch the existing structures to the limit: he was
rowing a boat that was leaving its moorings and heading for the

open seas, even as he kept an eye on the docks and sincerely believed he was merely heading out into a local, landlocked lake. Rowan Williams has a telling comment on Wesley's predicament:

> Thank God even for the eighteenth century Church of England, so clueless about how to handle a man so irresponsibly devoted to God that it *forced* him to wandering and exploration, folly and blundering, *and* unshakeable witness to full and free grace.

Chapter 3
The people called Methodists

The failure of renewal movements

John Wesley and his preachers set out 'to reform England, especially the church, and to spread scriptural holiness throughout the land'. This was the initial agenda of Methodism as a renewal movement in the Church of England. Like most renewal movements in the history of Christianity, it did not succeed. Instead it morphed into a network of Methodist denominations across the world.

This development is no surprise in the history of the church. Renewal movements often fail. This too should not surprise us, for the opportunities for error are manifold. Renewal movements generally involve a diagnosis of what has gone wrong, a prescription for fixing what has gone wrong, and a set of strategies for implementing the relevant prescription. These alone provide plenty of room for error. The diagnosis may be mistaken, the prescription wrong-headed, and the strategies misdirected. The response of the host church is equally important. It may or may not welcome the medicine offered.

Interestingly, one of the partial success stories of renewal in the history of the church is represented by the monasticism of the 2nd and 3rd centuries. I sometimes think of Methodism as monasticism for dummies, given the historical linkages and affinities between them. In the case of monasticism, Athanasius, a 4th-century theologian and bishop, brilliantly negotiated a settlement whereby the fruits of one of the greatest youth movements in the history of the church were harvested, albeit in a world within a world. This pattern was picked up in the Western Catholic tradition by the invention of various religious orders like the Franciscans or the Jesuits. In these instances renewal is only partially successful; it is essentially domesticated and contained within the body, becoming a new organ that feeds its gifts back into the body as a whole without remaking the body in its own image. Scholars have been tempted to see Methodism as a new Evangelical Order in the universal Church.

In the case of the Church of England, it is hard to discern why Methodism failed. In part the church was much healthier than Wesley realized; he had been wrong in his diagnosis. As such, then the prescription had been inappropriate and the strategies inept. The church certainly survived, just as she survived the renewalist efforts of John Henry Newman a century later. In the latter case, the Catholic revival in the Church of England took root and flourished well into the 1950s. Methodism never took root; in the end either indirectly forced out as an alien operation or leaving to go its own way. It was, as we say, six of one and half a dozen of the other.

A new version of Christianity

The bigger story here is that Wesley was inventing a whole new vision of Christianity that could not be contained within the sensibility and structures of the mother church. It is no accident that he spoke of wanting to restore real Christianity; or that he favoured the term 'Primitive Christianity' in application to the life and work of Methodism. These are radical notions, even though he presented them in terms that downplayed their revolutionary consequences. Wesley railed against outward religion; his mission was to restore inward religion, represented by the life of God planted within the depths of the human heart. However, he well knew that inward religion without outward forms is an illusion. To the contrary, he believed in the outward institutions and practices of the church; and he invented new institutions and practices to supplement those he inherited from his Anglican heritage. In turn the drive to restore inward religion inevitably exploded into an outward mission that led him to take steps that made it impossible for him and his followers to continue their membership in the Church of England. Even before he died he had founded a new Christian denomination in the New World; after he died his followers in Britain gradually drifted into their own existence as a church and ceased to be a network of fellowship groups.

All this happened despite a long-standing emotional and intellectual aversion to separation. Wesley died and was buried as a faithful member of the Church of England. Interestingly, unlike his brother Charles, he was not buried in ground consecrated by the church; he was quietly buried in his London headquarters in City Road. There is an ironic and dissonant symbolism in this marking of the end to his earthly labours: it was as if he and what he stood for had stepped out of the Church of England and into another world.

Wesley believed that he and his followers had been led into a wider world by God. This was not for him pious exaggeration or preaching. Consider one summary he provided.

> Let us observe what God has done already. Between fifty and sixty years ago, God raised up a few young men, in the University of Oxford, to testify those grand truths, which were then little attended to: – that without holiness no man shall see the Lord; – that this holiness is the work of God, who worketh in us both to will and to do; – and that he doth it of his own good pleasure, merely by the merits of Christ; – that this holiness is the mind that was in Christ; enabling us to walk as he also walked; – that no man

can be thus sanctified till he be justified; – and, that we are justified by faith alone. These great truths they declared on all occasions, in private and in public; having no design but to save souls from death.

From Oxford, where it first appeared, the little leaven spread wider and wider. More and more saw the truth as it is in Jesus, and received it in the love thereof. More and more found 'redemption through the blood of Jesus, even the forgiveness of sins.' They were born again of his Spirit, and filled with righteousness, and peace, and joy in the Holy Ghost. It afterwards spread to every part of the land, and a little one became a thousand. It then spread into North Britain and Ireland; and a few years after that in New York, Pennsylvania, and many other provinces in America, even as far as Newfoundland and Nova Scotia. So that, although at first this 'grain of mustard seed' was 'the least of all the seeds;' yet, in a few years, it grew into a 'large tree, and put forth great branches.'

There is no mention here of the churchly developments that provided the transition. Spiritual life is indeed inward, subjective, personal, and invisible to the physical eye. However, it needs outward forms to carry it across space and time. This principle was burned into Wesley by his own experience. Without his formation in Anglican church life and without the encounter with Moravian missionaries and practices there would have been no large Methodist trees with great branches. Equally, sustaining inward religion depended on external forms. The development of these forms was pivotal in the creation and growth of Methodism. As constructed within Methodism they not only made it the renewal movement it became, they caused its separation from the mother church, and they enabled Methodism to become the new network of denominations it became. Without Wesley realizing it, they upended his plans for renewal. Wesley wanted reform and renewal; what he got was a new church. One set of instruments that led from renewal to church can be found in the institutional innovations he himself undertook in the interest of his mission to save souls from sin and death.

Consider what it takes to move from an association within a church to actually becoming a church. Churches can readily tolerate and even welcome all sorts of associations within them such as bible study groups, missionary societies, theological guilds, youth movements, and the fellowships of noble organists. Methodism was much more than these in its aims and practices: it was a movement obsessed with salvation. Now salvation is not just one more item on the agenda of the church, it is central to its very life. Methodists set out to save souls, understood in a comprehensive sense as nothing less than the recreation of human agents in the image and likeness of God. The hidden implication at this point is that the church of the day must therefore be falling down in this critical enterprise. In fact, as Methodists saw it and said it out loud, its clergy and members were themselves desperately in need of salvation. Suppose the rank and file and the leadership were to reject this assessment. Suppose further that Methodism partially succeeded in its mission. There was then the obvious danger that Methodism would in the name of its mission take on a whole new and separate life of its own. This is precisely what happened. All that was needed was the actions signalling that the deed was done; with this a line had been crossed and there was no way back.

Wesley from the very beginning was headed towards that line. Being ordained as a priest, he had authority to make use of the practices of the church to save souls. Thus he could preach and administer the sacraments, the normal channels for making the grace and mercy of God available. Even then, early on he began to innovate. He preached in other clergy's parishes, proclaiming triumphantly that the whole world was his parish. He started preaching out of doors in the open air. He brought lay assistants on board to preach in order to multiply the effort of sowing the Gospel seed. He gathered the converts into small groups and knit them into a single group. He formed Annual Conferences with his helpers to make decisions on where to go, what to teach, and how best to further the work of God. He developed rules for membership, legally registered his buildings with the government, and established doctrinal standards. He adopted disciplinary procedures for dealing with wayward members and preachers. He invented special midnight services, love feasts (special meetings for singing and testimony), and covenant services. He had his followers sing a body of distinctive, memorable hymns. He held communion services with groups so large that he had to ask his brother to come up with new hymns on the spot for those attending to have something edifying to do as they waited their turn to receive the body and blood of Christ. In effect he was creating what has been called *ecclesiae* in *ecclesia*, that is, little churches within the church. The shift to becoming a church in its own right was an accident waiting to happen. And when it did, Wesley, intoxicated with a sense of divine mission, saw it as a work of providence.

Even so, all this could have been contained within the boundaries of the Church of England if he had not crossed the line between movement and church. That line was crossed in the ordination of some of his preachers into the priesthood. At this point there was no need for a grand theory of church identity to know that they then had a new church on their hands. At this point the water had been spilt and it could not be gathered up again. When Wesley took the decision to ordain, this was no trivial matter, nor was the decision taken lightly. The problem he faced was acute because he believed passionately in the place of the Lord's Supper in the transmission of grace and the cultivation of life-giving faith. In order to secure proper practice in this arena, he needed proper ordination. Later Methodists would fail to see the dilemma Wesley faced intellectually. E. Stanley Jones, an evangelist and teacher beloved across the globe in later Methodism, can serve as an example:

> When the question of the validity of orders and successions is being discussed I find myself falling asleep. I am simply not interested. It is all so irrelevant. For here at Pentecost the highest was open to a person as a person, and Peter and James and John stood in a

position not one whit different from the humblest seekers and believers. The Holy Spirit was given alike to all and this directly and immediately without the intervention of anyone.

The search of succession

Wesley took issues of orders and succession deadly seriously. He had inherited the doctrine of apostolic succession which declared that valid orders came physically through the laying on of hands by those who could trace their own ordination back to the apostles and Jesus. However, he rejected the doctrine on the basis of his reading of the works of theologians of his day who had worked to undermine this pipeline theory of succession. Even so, the sacred effects of this doctrine seemed to linger in his heart and soul. As we have already seen, he sought out the services of a wandering Eastern Orthodox bishop to ordain some of his preachers. He was clearly looking for someone who stood in the physical line of apostolic succession when he did this. This was an ill-conceived scheme for several reasons. While technically it might be correct—the right hands were used—the ordinations were completely divorced from their proper context within the Orthodox Church. Furthermore, those ordained were not Orthodox. And they were going to operate under the authority of Wesley rather than the authority of the good bishop from Crete. It all fell apart when some of his own hothead preachers sought out the services of the same bishop and paid for his labours. The whole matter was quietly dropped; it was an embarrassment that was long denied by some of the best historians of Methodism.

Wesley, however, did not at all abandon ideas of order or succession as essential for the administration of the Lord's Supper. The issue came to a head when he tried to solve the problem of the sacraments for Methodists in North America. After the North American colonies became independent, there were no Anglican clergy to serve communion. One of the first pioneers in the field there, William Strawbridge from Ireland, had already decided to administer the sacrament of the Lord's Supper as a preacher and layperson. The issue could well have led to chaos and fragmentation. Wesley took the matter quite literally into his own hands. However, this was not before he had convinced himself that there was no distinction between presbyters and bishops in the New Testament. As a properly ordained presbyter he was in reality a bishop; so he had the authority to ordain. He did so both for the work in North America and for areas in the homeland where Methodists could not get access to the sacraments. While this made perfect sense to Wesley as a logician, it made little sense to others, most especially his brother, Charles. However, Charles had long become a marginal figure in the movement, and John was not exactly meek and docile once he had made up his mind.

Ordination was but one step in the process of forming a new Christian denomination. Churches need not only orders of ministry like deacons, elders, and bishops, they also need doctrinal standards, forms of worship, systems of discipline, and a common mission. All of these elements were already developed; they had been tried and tested for a generation and more while Methodism was still a movement. It was easy to pick them up and transfer them into a Methodist church. Equally important, a church needs a mechanism for making decisions about these matters and for making adjustments about life together in the future. Among the first Christians the mechanism used had been that of an assembly or a conference, as is recorded in Acts 15. This became the model for later assemblies known as Ecumenical Councils. Methodism took up this mechanism, understanding that it was not a mere human assembly but one where the church looked to the Holy Spirit to give wisdom and direction. In this way a church can survive the deaths of its current leaders, resolve disputed questions, express a unity that transcends its local communities, and secure continuity and succession across space and time.

Some Christians have looked upon these developments as a fall into institutionalism. They lead, they would say, to exactly the kind of outward religion that inhibits the growth of inward religion. Wesley did not share this conviction. He agreed that lots of Christians were tempted to restrict religion to nominal membership and outward forms. However, the solution was to restore the proper balance between the inward and the outward, the personal and the social. One of the hallmarks of Methodism has been the enormous energy that is spent in taking care of outward forms. They have a passion for keeping statistics. They borrow religious forms and practices developed by others and they invent their own. They have by nature been methodical and pragmatic, constantly seeking out what will work to serve the interests of mission. They have loved things to be done decently and in order. Yet they have also been hearty supernaturalists who look to the Holy Spirit to animate the outward forms and practices and thus bring new life to those who come to them seeking the face of God.

Sanctified flexibility

The commitment to pragmatism is very much in evidence in the choice and appointment of leaders. This is not just a matter of human judgement, it is also derived from a very important theological decision. There is a common core of persons and practices that are non-negotiable. Thus Methodists insist on the sacraments of baptism and Eucharist; and they insist on orderly ordination for their clergy. But beyond that there is flexibility, innovation, and adaptability. While they defend the practice of baptism and Eucharist as mandated by Christ himself, they note that the New Testament does not lay down any blueprint for exact orders of ministry. The Bible is only authoritative for matters relative to salvation; it manifests broad principles for the orders of ministry and beyond that leaves the church to make prudent decisions aided by the Holy Spirit. Hence it insists on a spiritual call to church work and on competence to preach and lead. This relatively broad outlook is one reason why Methodists have been able to ordain women with minimum fuss and little or no division.

This flexibility can be readily illustrated by comparing orders of ministry in Britain, in the United States, and elsewhere. British Methodism has never had bishops. In its gradual separation from the Church of England, it has invented the office of district superintendent; certain leaders are appointed but not ordained to oversee a region for a time before they return to local ministry. For the Annual Conferences, there is a president of the conference who provides leadership for one year and then steps aside. In the United States, from the beginning, Methodists adopted the threefold distinction between deacon, elder, and bishop. Even then bishops were not ordained to a third order of ministry; they were consecrated with special functions in the church as a whole. Amazingly, bishops were not given a vote in the General Conferences which meet every four years to govern the life of the church. Their job is to preside. Bishops sometimes joke that they are essentially like flower pots: their job is to sit on platforms, be quiet, and look good. Outside the United States one can find bishops who are only elected for limited terms; they have to be re-elected every four years and must step down after twelve. This is clearly a variation on the North American model. In one case, Singapore, there is a complex synthesis of the British and North American models with presidents for each of the Annual Conferences and a bishop for the General Conference when the whole church is represented.

Core elements

These differences of personnel and polity do not override the non-negotiable elements that have become central to Methodists throughout the world. Every Methodist church will have lay members and clergy; it will have the sacraments of baptism and Eucharist; it will have formal and informal practices of worship; it will have a designated body of hymns; it will have books of doctrine and discipline; and it will have courts and canon law for conducting trials of members and clergy. For the most part, clergy will be appointed rather than called to their local church; and they will serve under the orders of bishops or of stationing committees. Most important of all Methodists will meet on a regular basis in Annual Conferences and, where needed, General Conferences. This is where ultimate authority lies for exercising oversight over the church as a whole. Clergy have their membership in an Annual Conference rather than a local church.

I know of no analogous body that can command so effectively the affection and loyalty of its members. It is hard to capture the devotion that membership in these conferences evokes. Being mistreated by one's Annual Conference is as painful as being betrayed by one's biological family. Being honoured by appointment to leadership is sought and coveted as much as leadership is coveted in any social organization.

Two further features of these elements of church life deserve mention. First, they provided ample ways of creating new Methodist bodies. When African-American Methodists led by Richard Allen (1760–1831) and Absalom Jones (1760–1831) initially walked out of their church in Philadelphia in 1787 after they had been banned to the galleries, they could immediately form a church of their own; the blueprint was already to hand (Figure 3). Take another example. Suppose a group of Christians in China or in Vietnam have come to faith, heard about Methodism, and want to become Methodists. The formula is simple. They form a local congregation; they contact Methodist leaders in the region; once they have several congregations, they form a provisional conference. After that they adopt the standard practices of Methodism and eventually are given full autonomy in their own Annual Conference. They are then free to join the World Methodist Council.

Second, at their best these standard elements in the life of the church provide the space for the emergence of not just bonds of unity and loyalty but of inimitable warmth, friendship, camaraderie, and faith. Even in the midst of heart-breaking

3. Richard Allen postage stamp.

disagreements and disputes there is a sense of belonging to each other that is extraordinary. This was especially nurtured in the early periods by the intensity of the singing, by conversations and testimonies around the kitchen table in the home, in the hearing of the Word of God presented with deep conviction in the preaching, and in the common suffering and fellowship of sharing the Gospel in word and deed.

Modern Methodism and renewal movements

Across the years the outward forms I have just described have remained essentially intact. So too has much of the ethos and sensibility that animated them in the first place. Yet the problems that beset the mother church have shown up again within Methodism, especially in the West. New renewal movements have sprung up inside and outside of Methodism to challenge it in ways that mirror some of the ways Methodism itself challenged the Church of England. Consider the drive to attain organic unity across the face of Christendom and the civil rights movement in the United States. Both have roots within Methodism. The ecumenical movement set out to fix the problem of disunity; the civil rights movement tackled the moral problem of racism. The fruits of these two movements have been gladly harvested. Thus Methodists have been deeply involved in the ecumenical movement worldwide. In the United States the efforts to overcome the sin of racism remain unabated.

Contrast this attitude with the response to three homegrown renewal movements in the United States: the Good News movement, the Confessing movement, and the Mission Society for United Methodists. In recent years the first two have functionally merged to work on a common agenda of doctrinal, evangelistic, and moral renewal; the third has been committed to planning new churches across the globe. Not a single bishop or network of leaders has welcomed this work. There has been no corporate interest in harvesting the fruits of these groups comparable to the fruit of the ecumenical movement or the civil rights movement. For the most part there has either been silence or hostility. The story of the response to a third renewal movement is fascinating. The charismatic movement which stresses full life in the Holy Spirit in terms of both experience and gifts is one of the most important renewal movements in 20th-century Christianity. It has deep roots within Methodism from which its history can be traced. In Britain, Europe, and the United States, the response has been lukewarm at best. Elsewhere, across South America, in Costa Rica, Cuba, Africa, and Singapore, the response has been exceptionally positive. I see this development as a critical recovery and updating of what Methodism was in its origins as a movement and its later embodiments as a church. However, to make sense of this judgement we need to look at the message of Methodism across the centuries.

Chapter 4
The message of Methodism

An ambitious vision

Methodism is not a cult of John Wesley, it is a whole new vision of Christianity. While it clearly bears the imprint of John Wesley and the early leaders, it had to develop the doctrinal and intellectual resources to carry it across space and time. Its initial message was certainly furnished by Wesley, but it was not limited to Wesley. Moreover, given its mission to spread Christianity near and far, it necessarily made adjustments as best it could as it spread across the world.

I am thinking of 'message' here in broad terms; it refers to the complex network of doctrines that became essential to the teachings and identity of Methodism. It is important to understand the range of materials deployed. Think of the whole as a building with a set of rooms and ample basements. On entry into the spacious hallway one sees the soaring walls and the heavy pieces of classical furniture that contain the great doctrines of incarnation and Trinity developed in the early church and assumed at the Reformation. Beyond that one enters a cosy living room where the guest is presented with those intimate doctrines that bring the mercy and love of God into the human heart. Downstairs in the basement there is an effective system for streaming the fresh air of grace throughout the building, with air-conditioning available in the summer and heat in the winter. Below that there is another level where the architectural and building plans have been stored. These display the intellectual grounding represented by scripture, revelation, and other highbrow goods that give the building as a whole defences against infiltration from termites and dangerous reptiles.

Christian communities construct buildings like this as a corporate enterprise. In Methodism the building began by taking material already available and adding materials provided by its founder. However, this represented no mere individual decision on the part of Wesley; what he proposed was taken up and ratified by the people who went on to be called Methodists. Thus the theological teachings adopted were official; they were not just the property of Wesley. They were canonical in the sense that they were publicly listed and thus made available for public inspection and ownership. Without them Methodism would quickly have degenerated into a Protestant sect or a loose band of local communities without any common identity or mission.

In early British Methodism, given that it was still part of the Church of England, there was no need to specify what was already given by the mother church. On separation from the Anglican womb in the early 19th century there was an aborted effort to develop a set of Articles of Religion, but the job was never finished. In the case of North America, Wesley provided an abridged version of the Thirty-Nine Articles, making it abundantly clear that he intended that there be a serious church with specific and identifiable doctrine. Each Article picked out an individual item of Christian teaching. Even so these had to be ratified officially; with the addition of one new Article on the relation between the church and the civil authorities, they became the canonical doctrine of the Methodist Episcopal Church. In the British case, the canonical doctrines were identified as Wesley's *Standard Sermons*, his *Notes on the New Testament*, and a set of *General Rules*. Interestingly, it appears these were never officially adopted by the Methodists in

North America; there they attained the persuasive force of tradition rather than the force of legal enactment. We might call this material the distinctive message of Methodism despite the difference in official standing in the two major streams that developed.

We now know what was in the spacious lobby and the living room. As to the architectural and building plans, these were sparse indeed, being limited to a carefully worded Article on scripture and a set of relatively informal proposals scattered here and there in *Standard Sermons* and the *Notes on the New Testament*. These wobbled between a more cautious appeal to scripture in the Article, on the one hand, and a pretty hardline doctrine of inerrancy in the Wesley material, on the other. There is a solid appeal to scripture as the critical grounding of Methodist doctrines. However, this appeal was taken in an inclusive sense in that it allowed reference to tradition, reason, and experience, but only as confirmation and not as an independent set of norms. Behind this vision stood the appeal to special revelation mediated in scripture, a commonplace in Western Christianity. Behind it also stood the clear intention to allow for revision of all doctrine provided the appropriate official procedures were followed. Methodism was thus from the beginning a conciliar denomination that looked to church conferences to make the necessary adjustments; the church as a whole through its elected representatives will make decisions rather than, say, local congregations or a council of bishops.

Methodism made next to no contribution to a fresh verbal statement of the classical doctrines of the Christian tradition such as incarnation, atonement, and Trinity. This material was sung more than it was recited and interpreted. John's treatment, say, in the *Standard Sermons*, is ad hoc and limited. Charles's treatment is extraordinary in its poetic expression and articulation. Consider a sample picked at random on the incarnation:

> He laid His Glory by,
> He wrapped Him in our clay;

Unmarked by human eye
The latent Godhead lay.
Infant of days He here became,
And bore the mild Immanuel's name.

Consider a second sample on the significance of the death of Christ:

O Love Divine what has thou done?
The immortal God has died for me.
The Father's co-eternal Son
Bore all my sins upon the tree.
The immortal God for me has died,
My Lord, my Love is crucified.

The canonical sermons

One neat way to understand the distinctive material of the canonical sermons is to look at how Wesley organizes the content of his *Standard Sermons*. These forty-four sermons are divided naturally into three conspicuous units.

The first fifteen provide an overview of how one becomes a genuine Christian as opposed to a nominal member of the church. They describe what salvation is, how it is obtained, and where it will lead. The inquiry is given the conceptual tools that are needed to map the experiences of faith, repentance, assurance, and genuine victory over evil. They end with a sermon on how the manifold grace of God—understood as the generosity and power of God—is mediated through practices such as prayer, the study of scripture, and the Lord's Supper.

The second batch of thirteen work through the Sermon on the Mount in Matthew 5–7and provide a summary of what it is to be a Christian. It had been common at this point to cover material like the Ten Commandments and the Lord's Prayer. Wesley replaced these with the more apt material covered in the Sermon on the

Mount. He works through the requirements of inward and outward religion, making clear that the fruit of true faith is the radical transformation of the human person.

The third group of sixteen pulls together a network of challenges that one will meet should one become a Christian in the Methodist tradition. They begin with the danger of abandoning the written law of God and end with prosaic advice on what to do with money. Both are serious problems. Given the stress on inward religion there is a danger of casting aside public revelation in favour of personal desires and moral illusions; and given that Methodists are liable to be hard-working they are in danger of being carried away by the lust to make money. In the former case, Wesley develops a subtle view of moral teaching imparted in divine revelation through conscience, the prophets, and most fully through Christ. In the latter case, he suggests a simple rule: make all you can, save all you can, and give all you can. In between he works through a laundry list of other challenges: the danger of fanaticism and bigotry, the possibility of overestimating the quest of perfection and underestimating the ravages of sin, the problem of spiritual dry spells and spiritual depression, the readiness to avoid suffering, and the ever-present temptation to gossip.

Crucial elements

Let us look at a raft of crucial elements in Wesley's teaching.

Consider his take on justification by grace through faith and not through works. Given that Wesley held to a deep doctrine of original sin, the challenge was how to get right with God. For many the solution was to do the best one could and hope that God would allow one's moral endeavours and successes to count favourably against one's sins and vices. The good news on this front was that this had things back to front. God had come to the world in Christ, paid whatever price sin merited, and was delighted to welcome us home on the basis of repentance and faith. To be sure, this was not easy to accept. However, faith was in turn an additional gift given to those who sought it; and even that effort was divinely assisted. So seek and find; and then go on to make faith visible by works of love.

Justification is accompanied by new birth. Where the language of justification came from the law courts, this language came from the maternity ward. In returning to God, the Holy Spirit began to take possession of believers so that they could start their lives again. Often this experience was instantaneous; just as there is a time of existence before babies are born, their actual birth occupies a specific time and place. However, the analogy should not be pressed too far; and God works in us in ways individual to each one of us, even in infants brought to baptism with no idea what was happening.

All being well, the coming of the Holy Spirit in new birth is a conscious experience. The convert had a sense of assurance, an inner witness of the Spirit that was different from such witness as one could garner by checking for the marks of the Spirit in love, joy, and peace. The language once more returns to that of the law courts. There is a divine witness in the heart that is analogous to a court witness who must speak the truth about what has happened in an incident being adjudicated. Spoken of in terms of faith, believers are given new spiritual senses akin to ordinary senses that enable them to perceive the love of God made visible in Christ. This faith is not some generic hoping for the best; it is faith directed to Christ in all his offices as prophet, priest, and king. This faith comes by hearing; it is not something worked up emotionally. It comes as a gift rather than a human achievement even though it depends on human attention and assent.

This assurance was not an end in itself. The ultimate goal was nothing less than being made perfect in love for God and neighbour, here and now. Wesley had a range of concepts to hand at this point: he borrowed the language of Christian Perfection from the ancient tradition of the church. He also spoke of entire sanctification, a high-octane notion that suggested an all-out commitment to God without reservations. At other times he used concepts relating to holiness of heart and life, purity of intention, all the mind that was in Christ, circumcision of the heart, and a renewal of the human person in the whole image of God. More often than not, given the initial concerns about guilt and assurance that beset the new convert, it took time for this gift of grace to sink in. Entering into this kind of experience and new life could be as big a crisis as one's initial conversion and new birth. Whatever the case psychologically and temporally, there was never a time when one did not need the forgiving grace of God. The ultimate goal of sinless perfection was to come in life beyond the grave.

For Wesley these critical themes are the outcome of the all-pervasive grace of God understood in terms of divine generosity directed to sinners who bear the marks of original sin, and in terms of divine power which unleashes moral energy within the human agent. Later writers summarize this element in terms of a dramatic outpouring of prevenient, justifying, and sanctifying grace. Prevenient grace is the grace that comes before, readying the human agent to consent to the gift of grace that would bring forgiveness (justifying grace), then followed up by the grace which would enable one to gain victory over evil (sanctifying grace). Expressed in terms of the Gospels, Wesley is capturing the theme of the arrival of the Kingdom of God through the work of Christ and the Holy Spirit. It speaks of divine life—eternal life—entering initially into history from God the Father through the Son and the Spirit and now realized to an astonishing degree in human hearts and lives.

One further theme deserves mention, namely, that of predestination. It is commonly thought that Wesley was opposed to the whole idea of predestination. However, while at times he worked from the definition of predestination found in Calvin and his disciples, he did vehemently reject their notion of predestination. Calvin held that God had predetermined from all eternity to save some particular individuals to salvation and that the rest were intentionally destined for damnation. For Calvin this was crucial for defending the doctrine of justification by grace through works; any reference to human action would mean that salvation was not by grace. Wesley shared the need to secure salvation by grace through faith. However, this did not mean he abandoned the idea of predestination. He believed God had predestined those who believed to be saved; and predestined that those who did not believe would not be saved. Predestination was directed to groups not to lists of individuals. In fact this version of predestination safeguarded the mercy of God, for God had to have mercy on those who came in simple faith to Christ, while he hardened those who stubbornly resisted; this was not some human decision or policy. Moreover, given the Fall into sin and spiritual death, God made it possible to say 'yes' to justifying grace through the preparatory grace that made it possible for sinful human agents to consent to faith as a gift of God. Predestination and grace were compatible with human freedom.

In terms of academic theology Wesley is here making his own unique contribution to what is called ascetic theology. The Protestant term for this was practical divinity or piety; the modern term is spirituality. Thus it is a serious mistake to overheat his contribution and turn him into the kind of theologian who provides a careful articulation of the full contours of Christian theology. This does not mean that Wesley and the early Methodists did not care about the great themes of Christian theology; they are clearly represented in the official hymnody of British Methodism and, additionally, in the Articles of Religion in North American Methodism. Wesley's theological gifts for better or worse lie elsewhere; he is essentially a theologian of Christian experience and the Christian life. The great challenges across space and time have been twofold: holding all of the official teachings initially as a single whole; and subsequently preserving them as essential elements of Christianity as presented afresh in Methodism.

Industrial strength theologies

With the transition from renewal movement to a distinct network of Methodist churches, the development of full-scale theologies that cover the great themes of Christian teaching was inevitable. This happened in both Britain and North America, the two great centres of Methodism in the 19th century. Even though British Methodism remained a minor affair in its homeland, it produced two comprehensive articulations of Methodist teaching in the works of Richard Watson and William Burt Pope. Both sets of volumes were scholastic in tone and content; they were clearly works of defence and positive interpretation. There was a much greater crop in North America once the Methodist universities were launched. Drew University in Madison, New Jersey and Vanderbilt University in Nashville were especially productive, even as they were eclipsed by the first institution of higher learning at Boston University. Two of the best productions are worth mentioning: the three-volume work by Thomas O. Summers at Vanderbilt and the splendid and lengthy one-volume work by Henry Sheldon at Boston. This represented a golden period of Methodist dogmatic theology understood as a learned and rigorous statement of full-dress Christian teaching.

Contrary to popular worries and much opposition within the ranks of Methodist evangelists this intellectual outpouring did not inhibit the spiritual vitality of Methodism. Developing the life of the mind did not undermine the enthusiasm of the heart. The desire for spiritual vitality was captured in the tradition of revivals that were brilliantly co-opted by Francis Asbury and became standard fare in that tradition. It was this aspect of Methodist revivalism that was exported to other parts of the world. A great era of intellectual endeavour that sought to plumb the depths of Methodist reflection, experience, and practice was an aid rather than a barrier to growth and mission. In this its scholars, utterly devoted experientially to the earlier heritage, were following in the footsteps of Wesley and the first generation as represented by Wesley himself, and by figures like Adam Clarke (1760–1832) and John Fletcher (1729–85). Fletcher, originally from Switzerland, produced a massive defence of the Methodist vision of predestination and perfection. Clarke, originally from Ireland, was something of a theological misfit who completed a six-volume commentary on scripture. He held that the snake in Genesis 3 was an orang-utan because it spoke to Adam and Eve; and he developed oddball views on the Trinity that denied the eternal procession of the Son from the Father. Later, intellectuals in Methodism worried about the orthodox content of the material; they also felt it was unsuited to new moral and intellectual challenges, and, as a result, they dismissed if not demonized this golden period as one of horrid scholasticism.

Initial updating of the message

One can see this concern for updating Methodist teaching already emerging in the later 19th century. Borden Parker Bowne (1847–1910), the undisputed intellectual leader at Boston University, had gone to Germany and picked up the new philosophical trends at play there. He was in two minds, for example, about miracles. He believed in the virgin birth and the resurrection, but he rejected any idea of divine intervention or direct divine action in the world. The effort to sort out this kind of dissonance was heightened with the arrival of the historical study of scripture and with new developments in natural science that called into question any idea of a literal Adam and Eve. The clash between new knowledge and the classical Methodist doctrines caused enormous headaches on both sides of the Atlantic. Add to that the challenge posed by the disputes and division over slavery, the ravages of industrialization, the pressure to bring Christian convictions into the market place, and the consequences of engaging other religions on the mission field,

and one can readily see that many leaders were forced to begin to
wonder if the traditional doctrines of Methodism either in whole
or in part were fit for purpose.

One remarkable figure, Harry F. Ward (1873–1966), left England
to become a street evangelist in Utah. He developed a passion
for socialism after working in rat-infested slums where he changed
the call to commitment in his evangelistic meetings to a call to
join the local trade union. In time he became an ardent socialist,
reinterpreting Jesus as a carpenter and thus a splendid member
of the working class, and looking to communism in Russia as the
arrival of the kingdom of God. He also climbed the academic
ladder, moving from Boston University to Union Seminary, where
he was completely eclipsed by the person and work of Reinhold
Niebuhr (1892–1971), one of the premier moral thinkers of the
20th century. Ward founded the American Civil Liberties union.
He was on the watch list of the FBI; on his 90th birthday in 1966
he received a congratulatory telegram from the great atheist and
activist Bertrand Russell for his political radicalism.

In this instance the message of Methodism had clearly become
something very different from what had been handed over by
Wesley and officially adopted by Methodist churches. However,
rank and file clergy still subscribed to the canonical doctrines at
their ordination, as they do to this day, with many members still
picking up the essentials of the tradition. They remained convinced
of the truth, vitality, and relevance of Methodist teaching. Within
the tradition the Holiness movement, most effectively represented
by Phoebe Palmer (1807–74), a remarkable travelling evangelist
and teacher, sought to keep alive the faith of the fathers (Figure 4).
Its advocates wanted to keep in place Wesley's controversial teaching
on sanctification, even as they interpreted it in novel ways. Some
groups like the Free Methodists and the Church of the Nazarene
were either forced or left to leave and to recapture the Wesleyan
commitment to serve the poor. Yet others, following in part the
lead of Fletcher and of William Arthur (1819–1901), a remarkable

Ever Yours in love
Phoebe Palmer

4. Phoebe Palmer.

Irish autodidact, began to explore a Pentecostal aftermath or update to Methodism. They took up Wesley's views on sanctification, looked at them afresh in the light of Acts 2, and worked out a vision of baptism in the Holy Spirit that spread in time across the world. John Wesley now had spiritual grandchildren.

The crucial point to note here is that Methodism, with the rest of Christianity in the West, faced a formidable array of challenges to its originating message. Few, if any, thought of working to change official teaching. Perhaps the bar of constitutional change had been set too high, for it needed supermajorities to pass; perhaps the very process of securing change was seen as out of date; or perhaps there was enough trouble figuring out what to teach without wasting energy on bureaucratic and political exercises. It was enough to identify the crisis, make a passing nod to Wesley or to this or that element somewhere in the tradition, and get on with revising the inherited network of doctrines.

Chapter 5
The search for credible alternatives

Finding a viable alternative

The search for a viable alternative to classical Methodist teaching was taken up in earnest in the first half of the 20th century. If there was a failure of nerve in the effort to sustain the riches of the tradition, there was no lack of confidence in pursuing the quest for a better future intellectually. The basic strategy was to reach outside the boundaries of Methodism and find fitting materials that would replace the earlier orthodoxy. Some theologians and leaders looked to fresh work in biblical studies that in time would provide the material for new expressions of the Christian faith. Later this would be taken up in terms of a turn to Biblical Theology, a movement in North American that flourished in the 1940s and 1950s and sought to summarize afresh the message of scripture. Some turned to the material furnished by religious experience and borrowed from the great tradition of Liberal theology opened up in Germany by Friedrich Schleiermacher, a truly original thinker who was initially formed within a Reformed version of Pietism. Other influential figures in Methodism sought help from the extraordinary output of Karl Barth, whose writings were readily welcomed at Princeton Seminary and Yale Divinity School. Yale became something of a Mecca for a whole generation of Methodist scholars, not least Albert Outler (1908–89). Outler saw H. Richard Niebuhr of Yale, who had managed to work up a synthesis of Ernst Troeltsch—the last of the great line of German Liberal Protestants—and Karl Barth, as the greatest theologian of his generation. Others went to Boston University and the University of Chicago where they adopted the complex doctrines of Process Philosophy, a speculative vision of life as a whole invented by Alfred North Whitehead. Process Philosophy was especially attractive because it took seriously the suffering and passion of God, a theme dear to many Methodists.

In reaction to all of this, conservatives built Asbury Theological Seminary in Wilmore, Kentucky, in 1923 in an effort to provide a more faithful version of the Methodist message. Here the strategy was to seek resources in Fundamentalism and its later more moderate offspring in Evangelicalism, both of which stand in tension with the heart of Methodist theology and ethos. Wesley and Asbury were seen as the great exemplars and heroes of Methodism; the goal was one of retrieval and preservation, often in the teeth of opposition in Methodist circles. The most influential teacher there, Robert A. Triana, had been trained in systematic theology, but he mediated his profound insights through a study of scripture known as Inductive Bible Study. Many of the systematic theologians were conservative Evangelicals who read Wesley as a precursor of their own commitments. We might say that they interpreted the Methodist message as a form of Wesleyan Evangelicalism. The message of Methodism had become essentially a subdivision of a friendly but suspicious alien movement.

These developments did not mean the end of the originating Methodist message in its manifold dimensions. There remained throughout enormous affection for the figure of Wesley and for what he and the Methodist tradition had achieved across the years. The emphasis on personal experience of God, on practical service to the poor and needy, on winsome evangelism, on a catholic spirit in wishing well of other Christians, and on warm-hearted fellowship was still alive and well. Moreover, one can readily detect a conspicuous interest in salvation, most especially on the effects of salvation as shown in holiness. For conservatives, this interest took the form of the conscious experience of holiness, in conservative forms of dress and personal morality, and, in some cases, in aggressive efforts to abolish slavery. On the more progressive side, this interest went beyond the efforts to abolish slavery to work for the implementation of a Social Gospel that would Christianize the social order from top to bottom. Valiant efforts were made to connect these interests in personal and social salvation to the inherited doctrines. They have continued in place in updated forms even after there was little or no working consensus on how to think about them theologically.

The radical diversity of teaching came to a head in the 1960s in the work and impact of Albert Outler (Figure 5). He became, in time, the founding father of United Methodism, and the one scholar and teacher who was readily recognized as an international figure inside and outside of Methodism. He trained as a church historian at Yale, became a doyen of the ecumenical movement that sought organic unity across Christendom, and was an observer at Vatican II. He spent over thirty years editing the full corpus of Wesley's sermons: an astonishing feat of detailed scholarship. Most important of all, he was appointed to head the Theological Study Commission that was established to deal with the radical diversity that was visible throughout the most influential branch of Methodism.

He once described the situation that confronted the church in witty terms that indicated that somewhere in the United Methodist Church there is somebody urging every kind of theology still alive and not a few that are dead. His solution was manifold. First, embrace theological diversity as something good in its own right. Second, secure agreement on theological method by making a joint appeal to scripture, tradition, reason,

5. Albert Outler with the pope.

and experience, the warrants for theology. Third, get the whole
church, laity and clergy, to engage in theological reflection.
Fourth, include all of Wesley's sermons as standards of doctrine,
but treat them alongside all the other materials as landmark
documents that furnish relatively helpful material in our own
theological endeavours. Finally, take the theology developed
on the road in service to the world, translating it where needed
into the idiom of the host culture. The latter move was Outler's
way of updating what happened on the Day of Pentecost when
foreigners heard the good news of grace spoken in their own
tongues. These moves were not just approved by the colleagues
who worked with him, they were voted overwhelmingly to
become the official doctrines of United Methodism. Dissent from
these prescriptions was until recently greeted with significant
opposition. They became doctrinal litmus tests for clergy and
were disseminated throughout Methodism by its clergy and its
publishing arm.

It is not difficult to see what Outler had done. Using the study of Wesley as his leverage he had effectively baptized the intellectual chaos that had been embraced under the name of diversity and pluralism. He managed to get Wesley's sermons shoehorned into the official doctrines of United Methodism despite the fact that they had not appeared in the preceding editions of *Doctrine and Discipline*. Thus he jumped over the golden period of theology in the 19th century, treating it as a period of boring scholasticism unworthy of serious attention. Equally important, he had become convinced that the appeal to the quadrilateral of scripture, tradition, reason, and experience had solved the problem of authority for theology once and for all. He had in fact first worked this out in his conversations on church unity before applying it to the problem of division in Methodism. In this work he was—and he at times confessed this openly—an amateur in philosophy. Worse still, he had substituted an underdeveloped and naive theory of knowledge in theology as the heartbeat of Methodism. The official and working message of Methodism as worked out in the wake of the quadrilateral turned out to be a set of slogans about prevenient, justifying, and sanctifying grace. The dense content of the original materials had been sidelined and effectively eviscerated. It became a popular saying that Methodists believed anything and drank beer.

The pied piper of United Methodism

I knew Outler personally. He was an amazing raconteur; he would snow you with lists of books to be read; he was a brilliant public speaker; his essays are masterpieces; he had instant and interesting opinions on everything under the sun; and he was fearless in facing down critics. In the last years of his life, he deeply regretted some of the crucial decisions I have just enumerated. He developed serious misgivings about the quadrilateral. He regretted his railing against Christian orthodoxy, a theme in Wesley that he had never intended to have taken as a rejection of the great doctrines of the church. He thought that the material on the history of Methodist doctrine should never have been added to official church teaching. He even agreed that the official doctrines as represented by the Articles and Confession of Faith should have been left without comment, allowing readers to make up their own minds about them. He became so worried about the new theological fads that were being presented under the name of pluralism that he teamed up with one of the popular evangelists of the Evangelical Party to establish a fund for the training of evangelical scholars who might over time bring the ship back to its moorings in Wesley after its long search for an alternative theology.

Virtually none of this is known generally within Methodism. The only Outler Methodists really know is the Outler who became the founding father of Methodism. He was certainly happy with this state of affairs for a time. When a new doctrinal commission was set up to have another look at what he had engineered, I asked him what he thought of this. He told me without hesitation that in North America the Methodists had last looked at and adopted their official doctrines in 1808. That was over 150 years before they next took up the issue officially. Given the fine job that he and his colleagues had done there would be no more need to look at them again for another 150 years. Then he wondered aloud where they would ever get the scholars who could actually redo the work that he had effectively done. The change of mind that came several years later was a painful experience. It is a measure of his intellectual integrity that he frankly admitted his mistakes.

New directions

There have been interesting developments over the last fifty years. On the one hand, the diversity of voices has increased rather than decreased. The adoption of pluralism gave a green light to the creation of a host of caucuses and movements that have readily found a home in Methodism. James Cone (1936-2018) of Union Seminary, New York, pioneered the articulation of an African-American liberation theology. The theme of liberation was taken up at the Oxford Institute of Methodist Theological Studies in 1974 and remained the dominant melody until more recently when it was moved off into a subgroup. This meant that liberation theology, a vision of theology birthed in the Catholic Church in South America, became a heavily endorsed option globally across the Methodist family from Latin America to Asia. The Methodist message was at heart a political message of liberation for the poor and the marginalized. Methodist history was read through this lens and Methodist proposals on doctrine were to be examined for their contribution to this goal. Whatever ideas contributed to oppression was wrong; whatever ideas contributed to liberation was true. The writings of Wesley were ransacked for references to his concern for the poor. These were not difficult to find for they show up throughout his writing; in the latter stretch of his life Wesley was deeply worried about the effects of riches within Methodism. At one point he regretted that he had not imposed a dress code on Methodists and not required that excess wealth be brought to him for distribution. Over time, the identities of those who were to become the subjects of liberation multiplied. Feminist, Womanist, Hispanic, and Queer versions of Liberation theology have flourished. These were sometimes combined with earlier editions of professional theology developed in North America and Europe.

More recently, efforts to draw on postmodern ways of thinking have become popular. In this tradition the whole idea of objective reason is rejected; we are all caught in our own relative communities of meaning and value. This has been especially attractive to Methodist evangelicals who have been keen to find resources to attack the lingering remnants of Liberal Protestantism and to distance themselves from Fundamentalism. Other evangelicals have turned to Thomas Aquinas for inspiration. Thomas Oden (1931–2016) broadened this agenda to include the whole sweep of classical Christianity. Other Methodists have turned to the pacifist tradition because of the massive influence of Stanley Hauerwas, identified in 2001 as American's best theologian by *Time Magazine*.

Within this there has been a strong counter-cultural strain in Methodism that has relentlessly attacked the idea of the nation state and all forms of capitalism. Still others continue to burrow away in scripture, seeking to find a fresh rendering of a Christian theology that would be biblically based. They too had no difficulty in finding warrant for this in Wesley's work, given the place of scripture in the foundations of his theology. How far the results would fit with the official teachings of Methodism is and always will be an open question. In this respect the Protestant element in Methodism has its own unique role in adding to the list of options within Methodism. Another option for conservatives within Methodism has been to try to derive a full-scale theology in the writings of Wesley himself. The obvious danger here is that this turns Methodism into more or less a cult of Wesley and ignores the actual canonical doctrines that go way beyond what can be delivered directly in Wesley himself. In any case, Wesley has left us such a vast array of writings that the quest for the true Wesley theologically is something of a will-o'-the-wisp. Even when we find the true Wesley, there will be all sorts of proposals that are no longer credible given the information available to us today.

Pluralism prevails

The inevitable upshot of these developments is that any kind of survey of Methodists and their teaching on the ground will yield what had already been recognized in the 1960s, namely, no coherent message and no coherent body of doctrine. Whether we call it pluralism or whether we call it chaos is a matter of semantics. Whether Methodists like it or not, this is where they are. We can certainly find regional forms of consensus. Many Methodists in Latin and South America have taken on board elements of Pentecostalism; this is especially visible in Cuba and Costa Rica. It is also visible in Singapore and Malaysia. Much of African Methodism is still operating out of a version of 19th-century revivalism. This is also the case in South Korea, home to some of the largest Methodist congregations in the world. United Methodists on the East and West Coasts of North America are broadly committed to a progressive version of the tradition. In contrast, Methodists across the south of North America are more conservative in orientation. Many of the megachurches there have developed their own brand of Methodism. One of the most influential local churches is led by Adam Hamilton, a dazzling leader of a United Methodist megachurch in Kansas City, who has worked out his own appropriation of the tradition and been brilliant at sharing it with others through print and local conferences. Another figure, Kirbyjon Caldwell, a former Wall Street analyst, has provided a splendid updating of the African-American tradition in Methodism in Houston, Texas. We might say that on the ground the Methodist message has evolved into a network of contrasting and competing messages. There is a common ethos and a common origin, but no consensus. This is how things are in reality.

Queries about pluralism

Yet there is more to be said.

First, this situation mirrors what is happening across the board within Christianity in the West and worldwide. Even in the Roman Catholic communion, which projects a strong sense of unity to the world, there is enormous diversity of doctrine and practice. The same applies to the major branches of Protestantism in the West. There is a serious gap between what is professed on paper and what is actually believed and practised in reality. The challenges of modernity and now postmodernity have created differences within Christian denominations which in the premodern period showed up in differences between Christian groups. Now the differences occur within Christian groups. Thus some Christians within Methodism find themselves at times much closer to Christians within other denominations than they do to fellow Christians within Methodism.

Second, the massive effort to go back to Wesley was itself particularly worthwhile. It has resulted in a magnificent critical edition of Wesley's writings that can match what has long been available for other great figures like Aquinas, Luther, and Calvin. This effort initially trumpeted all sorts of optimistic promises which could never in fact be fulfilled. Yet the results have been salutary in enabling Methodists to take a fresh look at their identity and their intellectual resources. There is now a wealth of new scholarship that shows no sign of abating. This work has also given many a sense that they can hold their own in terms of offering resources to other Christian groups. There is less of an inferiority complex now than in the recent past.

Third, within Methodism there have been a host of renewal movements that have sought to retrieve crucial elements of the tradition seen as a whole. The most significant of these groups was the Confessing Movement which challenged the philosophical and historical assumptions that were central to the Outler agenda. Pluralism is an incoherent proposition. It claims to be inclusive, allowing everyone to come to the table with their own conclusions derived from the quadrilateral of scripture, tradition, reason, and experience. However, this requires the immediate exclusion of two groups within Methodism. It excludes those who reject the quadrilateral as an accurate reading of Wesley and, even more importantly, as a solution to long-standing issues related to authority. Given the extraordinary new developments in theory of knowledge, this is no trivial matter. Methodists who cling to the quadrilateral are simply behind the intellectual times. Equally important, it excludes those theologies that reject pluralism as hopelessly inadequate as a vision for the life of the church. The church is not some sort of eternal seminar, endlessly waiting to arrive at those truths that matter for salvation. Either God has given us access to these matters and we are capable of grasping them and canonizing them, or God is like an incompetent professor who never wants us to arrive at the truth. Wesley would never have endorsed the latter option.

Think about the issue this way. Even though many of us dislike politicians and politics, we take them seriously because their work is crucial to our welfare. They set tax rates, make laws, take us to war, regulate trade, make provision for the education of our children, and so on. We cannot be indifferent to what they believe and what they say. There is a clear parallel here with what we believe about, say, the person of Jesus and the salvation he offers. If we take the Christian faith seriously, its teachings are not trivial matters; they are matters of eternal life. If there is the kind of God that Methodists and Christians more generally say there is, then it would be bizarre for this God to leave us in the dark to fend for ourselves merely via our own speculations. Early Methodists both formally and informally insisted that we do have reliable access to the truth about God in the scriptures; that God has really reached out to us in effective revelation. We could be assured about the necessary conditions of being reconciled to God and of having the resources to live the holy life God planned for us from the beginning. Early Methodists faced a hostile world with a humble boldness that can only be explained by this kind of conviction. They articulated it with flair within and beyond the canonical heritage of their churches. However, all of this is utterly incompatible with the doctrine of pluralism as an essential mark of the church.

Fourth, once pluralism is defeated either by the weight of its own incoherence or by the intellectual chaos it engenders, the way is open for a revisiting of the originating message of Methodism as given in its canonical materials and practices. Recall what I said at the beginning of this chapter: Methodism is not a cult of John Wesley—it is a whole new version of Christianity. In the Methodist version of Christianity the only group that can speak for Methodists are those who gather in the relevant Conferences and decide what they officially believe and teach. Methodists meet in such conferences on a regular basis; they are the only representative body for their churches as a whole. These mechanisms or practices for making corporate decisions are not perfect; yet they are what they are and deserve the respect of both insiders and outsiders. The recent recovery of nerve on this front is a welcome sign of renewal, for this is a tried and tested way of sorting out the message that churches proclaim to the world. There are effectively no other options; and the precedent goes back to the days of the apostles.

Following this experimental line is not some kind of pious labour-saving device. In seeking to serve God in the present age, there will be lots of questions to ponder and answer. The very identity and reception of the message is itself an exercise in rigorous discernment. New rooms may need to be added to incorporate new insights into the canonical materials. Serious renovation may need to be conducted, not least in the area below the basement where theories of knowledge as they apply to theology are reviewed and invented. Some furniture may need to be removed. The task of developing full-scale systematic theologies will need to be taken up afresh with enthusiasm. Very hard choices may have to be made about the current challenges thrown up by debates about sexuality. There are no problem-free situations. Thus it has ever been in Methodism and thus it will ever be. Even if we solve the present disputes and problems, there will be others waiting up ahead. The apostolic identity and mission given to Methodism by the Holy Spirit remains in place; and there is every reason to believe that it can be executed with flair and confidence.

Chapter 6
The practices of Methodism

A crucial study tour

Shortly after his Aldersgate experience John Wesley embarked on a study tour of continental Europe. He was especially interested in visiting the Moravian communities whose members had such an impact on him both in Georgia and in England. The Moravians were not particularly impressed by this strange Englishman in their midst; they were not sure he was a real Christian and refused to allow him to participate in the Lord's Supper. Yet Wesley did not appear in the least annoyed at this. He was too busy sorting through the revolution that was bubbling up in his life.

On the one hand, he was still working through how best to understand what had happened to him. The Moravians had taught him to expect not just assurance about his salvation but also immediate victory over evil and persistent joy. In time the last two promises did not pan out; there was no immediate victory over evil and no persistent joy. The first remained a lasting element in his spiritual life, despite a short lapse in his middle years when he experienced a critical bout of scepticism about his status as a Christian. He wrestled for years on how best to think of new birth for himself and others.

On the other hand, Wesley had discovered that the rigid system of the first efforts at organizing Methodism at Oxford simply did not work in the New World. We might say that a second effort to make Methodism work failed and he was now looking for a third way to establish Methodism as an effective force for reform and renewal. Thus he was eager to observe what the Moravians believed and to examine their practices of prayer and spiritual formation that had been so effective in generating their confidence and their amazing missionary zeal. He had become an informal pragmatist in search of ways of expressing the evangelistic zeal that was jointly generated by his theological convictions and his new-found confidence. He was attending to the place of outward forms as they related to inward religion. He was exploring what social practices best served his desire to see holiness become a living reality in the nation and the church.

There was nothing especially original in the way that Wesley described what was at issue. He was exploring what he called the means of grace. In his canonical sermons this topic shows up third from last in the first set of sermons that explain what it is to become a Christian and helps prepare the way for the second set that explore what it is to be a Christian. The idea behind the means of grace is a simple one. Divine grace—God's generosity in forgiving sinners and God's energy in remaking them—does not generally come as a bolt from the blue. It is mediated through corporate practices. God can always choose to operate directly, as happened most dramatically in the conversion of the apostle Paul, but exceptions do not make for a rule. The rule is that God characteristically works through various means; hence the term 'means of grace'. There is nothing magical or superstitious at play here. God is the Creator who works in, with, and through the natural and human world. Divine agency is not limited to dramatic intervention; it can also work through ordinary human actions, say, baptism, and natural objects like bread and wine.

Means of grace

In the sermon 'The Means of Grace', Wesley mentions three means
of grace: prayer, searching the scriptures, and the Lord's Supper.
These are not optional practices in the life of the church; they are
absolutely necessary. They convey a myriad blessings on those
who approach them in the right spirit. Without them the life of the
church will be hopelessly impoverished. While Wesley's list is by
no means intended to be complete or comprehensive, it is notable
that it does not include baptism. This is strange because one way
to think of Wesley's approach to spiritual practices is to see it as
taking the classical means of grace developed in the church—most
especially through baptism and the Lord's Supper—and then
adding to them prudential means of grace that are invented,
dropped, and replaced as needed. Thus he developed small group
meetings for spiritual sharing and oversight; and he invented
special new year services where members reviewed the year that
was past and called for fresh dedication to God for the year to come
(known as covenant services).

Baptism and the Lord's Supper have a long history in Christianity
stretching back to Christ himself. In the West, Roman Catholicism
insisted over time on seven sacraments; Protestants cut them
back to two, arguing that these and these alone were instituted
by Christ. Both were outward and visible signs of inward and
invisible grace. With Wesley we find that his experience created
deep tensions with the traditional view of baptism. By contrast,
Wesley fully owned a very robust vision of the Lord's Supper. In
time, this configuration has been partially reversed. Many
Methodists have opted for a traditional vision of baptism without
any qualifications; simultaneously they have downgraded the vision
and place of the Lord's Supper in the life of the church. As far as
the prudential means of grace are concerned, the early Methodists
borrowed or invented a whole new battery of these; in time the
original ones have faded, replaced by other prudential means
of grace reflecting inevitable social and cultural changes.

However, the general pattern still holds: Methodists operate within the classical means of grace represented by baptism and the Lord's Supper, supplemented by a host of prudential means of grace that serve multiple purposes. These means of grace teach the faith, give occasion for repentance, make possible fresh commitment to God, provide encouraging forms of fellowship, and the like.

Baptism and the Lord's Supper

Let's look at baptism and the Lord's Supper.

Wesley followed convention in believing that in baptism the person baptized was born again of the Holy Spirit. This applied in the case of infant baptism, the practice that had become common in much of Christianity after the 4th century. The problem this practice generated is easy to understand. First, infant baptism seemed to have failed to deliver the goods in the lives of hosts of church members. Wesley took the standard line on this and said that folk sinned away their baptism over time. The solution to this problem was for nominal Christians to be born all over again without baptism. Others outside Methodism would say that the seed of new life was planted at baptism; this seed then needed to be watered and developed until a new rite of confirmation brought the seed to full flower. Many Methodists later opted for this solution.

Second, the account of new birth that Wesley developed, together with its associations with justification, assurance, and sanctification, made it strange to claim that new birth took place in the baptism of infants. Thus it is hard to see how babies could have any sense of assurance. While infant baptism was universally retained, the theory behind it was eroded. In much of later Methodism it effectively became a dedication service, a social occasion for families, or a point of entry to a social identity that was sceptical of the high-octane vision of the Christian life developed by Wesley. Clergy often spoke emphatically about infant baptism as providing an objective means of grace; however, the details were left vague compared to the conventional understanding of baptism as bringing about regeneration and new birth. In some Methodist denominations parents are free to choose between infant dedication and infant baptism, a practice allowed in the United Methodist Church because it was permitted in the Evangelical United Brethren, one of its forerunner denominations. For the most part this latter option has been aggressively suppressed. Moreover, any idea of Methodists opting for adult baptism after being baptized as infants has been vigorously rejected; the vigour bears witness to the fact that many Methodists have followed their theological conscience and broken quietly with standard practice.

The situation with the Lord's Supper has been the reverse of this. Early Methodists eagerly embraced a high vision of divine action in the Lord's Supper and were encouraged to participate as often as possible, preferably, for Wesley, once a week. Later Methodists for various reasons developed a much thinner version of divine action and moved to offer the Lord's Supper once a month.

Charles wrote a brilliant series of hymns on the Lord's Supper that emphasized the objective working of the Holy Spirit in transforming the bread and the wine into the body and blood of Christ. On the one hand, he rejected any idea of a literal miracle; on the other hand, he rejected any reduction of the sacrament to a mere memorial of the death of Christ. He insisted that the change brought about by God was essentially mysterious; not even the angels could explain what was happening. I recall seeing the informal effect of this vision as a boy in my local church, watching an older generation approach the sacrament. This was no trivial practice; some of their faces shone in quiet joy and expectation. They went forward to meet their risen Lord in his body and blood, and fully expected to be fed inwardly by the grace of God.

Charles Wesley nicely captured their quest and experience in this verse.

> Come Holy Ghost, Thine Influence shed,
>   And realize the sign;
> Thy life infuse into the bread,
>   Thy power into the wine.
> Effectual let the tokens prove,
>   And made by heavenly art,
> Fit channels to convey Thy love
>   To every faithful heart.

The sacrament of the Lord's Supper worked on many levels simultaneously: as a memorial of the death of Christ; as a sign and means of grace; as a pledge and foretaste of heaven; as a representation of the sacrifice of Christ; as a means for Christians to give themselves afresh to Christ.

It was difficult to sustain this high view of the Lord's Supper in Methodism. Early British Methodists relied on the Church of England to supply this service and were reluctant to move to administering it themselves. Initially, American Methodists had no clergy in place to offer the sacrament. Later, life on the frontier made it impossible to secure weekly administration. Later still, when commitment to divine action in the sacrament became less robust, there was a tendency to treat it as a memorial rite and a tendency to cut corners. The crucial element of repentance was watered down. The bread and the wine were often casually offered to anyone, without prior preparation or baptism. This latter practice is defended on the grounds that folk can be converted through the Lord's Supper, a theme that goes back to John Wesley himself. Sometimes this development comes across as a desire not to offend visitors and as an accommodation to a consumer society. Even so, the commitment to the Lord's Supper runs deep in the tradition across space and time.

Prudential means of grace

Beyond the use of the classical means of grace in the sacraments, early Methodists revelled in a network of supplementary practices that were crucial to its spread and survival. These have been named as prudential means of grace.

Think of the situation in the early days like this. Rosemary shows up reluctantly to hear a Methodist preach in the open air at 5.00 a.m., before going to work. She has already been baptized in the national church but rarely attends church, other than for marriages or funerals. She is awakened spiritually and begins to reflect on and question what she has heard. A Methodist close by notices this and invites her to come to a meeting the following week designed for seekers like her. On average it took seekers like Rosemary two years before they had any personal sense of assurance of the love and mercy of God; sometimes the search could last as long as four years. This journey from spiritual anxiety to spiritual relief involved listening to sermons, reading scripture, praying, talking to insiders, self-examination, fasting, singing hymns, and the like. If she was deemed to be serious, she would become a member of the Methodist Society in the area after a period of probation. Within the Society she would be assigned to a class meeting with an experienced leader. This class, of about a dozen members, would become a place of spiritual group direction. She would be asked questions about her soul; hear helpful testimonies from others on how they had come to faith; and be given instructions on how to move forward. These class meetings were absolutely crucial in the work of evangelism and spiritual formation.

Within this set up, she could in some places join a more select group, known as Bands, involved in a quest for the fullness of salvation through extremely intense forms of confidential, intimate sharing. These groups never really took off, but they were an important experiment that is currently being revisited.

She could also participate in special services known as Love Feasts where bread and water were served, and she could hear stories of spiritual awakening and encouragement. There might also be opportunities for Watch Night Services of praise and prayer. Early in each New Year there was a special Covenant Service where she would review the spiritual gains and failures of the previous year and make a full-throttle commitment to serve God in the following year. The climactic commitment ran as follows:

I am no longer my own, but thine.
Put me to what thou wilt, rank me with whom thou wilt.
Put me to doing, put me to suffering.
Let me be employed for thee or laid aside for thee,
exalted for thee or brought low for thee.
Let me be full, let me be empty.
Let me have all things, let me have nothing.
I freely and heartily yield all things to thy pleasure and disposal.
And now, O glorious and blessed God, Father, Son and Holy Spirit,
thou art mine, and I am thine.
So be it.
And the covenant which I have made on earth,
let it be ratified in heaven.
Amen.

The class meetings were the spiritual backbone of early Methodism and they lasted for over a century in both Britain and the United States. They remain a vital part of Methodism in some places even to this day. In South Korea they are held every Friday morning.

In North America a crucial additional practice emerged with the adoption of camp meetings and revivals (Figure 6). Camp meetings originated in Scotland among the Presbyterians after the Reformation as special communion services. They migrated to the North of Ireland and from there to the New World. These

6. Camp meeting in the USA.

naturally fitted the situation on the frontier, where folk would come together in a campground setting to be converted, be renewed in the faith, be baptized, and celebrate the Lord's Supper. Francis Asbury early on saw the potential for them and in typical Methodist fashion organized them from start to finish over a four-day period. Much of the time was taken up with a schedule of preaching and singing. Special hymnody developed that was much simpler in form and content than the more stately and theologically rich hymns that had become common in Methodism. The meetings followed a rhythm in which the intensity of the meetings reached a climax when the Lord's Supper was celebrated with great enthusiasm. Those who participated in these meetings often found themselves physically overwhelmed to the point where they would fall down, lose control of their limbs, burst into laughter, and take to dancing. Outsiders were quick to make fun of these phenomena. I have seen virtually all of these phenomena reproduced in what came to be known as the Toronto Awakening in the late 1990s. They were clearly psycho-physical in nature. Intense spiritual encounters with the divine led to startling physical effects. What mattered in the end was the spiritual transformation which followed.

When camp meetings were brought back to Britain, they were greeted with horror by establishment Methodists. They arrived at a time when British Methodists, led by Jabez Bunting (1779–1858), were keen to establish the pastoral office as a respectable office of control. This did not fit well with the more spontaneous, informal leadership that operated in the camp meetings. As a result a new Methodist denomination, the Primitive Methodist Church, was formed in 1811 by Hough Bourne (1772–1852) after he was expelled for promoting irregular forms of worship. Camp meetings flourished in the United States and continue in some settings to this day. There is an annual one in West Texas.

In time camp meetings were replicated in local churches in the form of revivals. These were akin to Lenten seasons spread over several weeks and held often twice a year. These remain popular in some rural areas and were exported in the missionary movement within Methodism that spread across the world. In some parts of Africa they have been domesticated to become the standing order for worship. In Ireland they were transformed into 'missions' which lasted for two weeks. They were held every three or four years and effectively became evangelistic meetings where nominal Christians were converted and many young folk came to a living faith.

Updating the system

The addition of these new practices did not initially mean the end of the class meetings. However, it proved difficult to sustain the class meetings over time. They required deft leadership and sustained attention. This was not always recognized, so they quietly died out, not being seen as important. In some instances they degenerated into an impotent form that did not achieve its original purpose of bringing revival. In North America, they disappeared after the ravages of the Civil War during which time church life had been severely disrupted. They were replaced by adult Sunday school classes which took on a whole new life of their own. These remain a vitally important part of church life even though there is little overall design to them. Some have sustained programmes of teaching; others function as places to meet friends and have fellowship. Many of them provide amazing informal services of care in times of bereavement and sickness. Adult Sunday school classes never took off in Britain, where it was assumed that the state would take care of religious education, restricting it to children and teenagers. In North America the state left religious education to the churches; Methodists readily moved to a model where education extended from cradle to the grave.

The most interesting effort to reinvent the class meetings took the form of covenant discipleship groups, where the idea of the class meeting was completely rethought by David Watson, an enterprising English Methodist who works in the United States. As an academic historian, Watson studied the early class meetings, tracing their history. He reconfigured them as a voluntary option rather than as required for membership. He updated the programme to an open-ended system of accountability and less as a place for conversion. The programme was officially adopted by the United Methodist Church and has taken root in some places. There have been other efforts to look again at the class meetings but nothing comparable has come of these efforts.

It is impossible to chart the richness of Methodists' inventiveness in all sorts of small groups. Not surprisingly, given the size and resources of the United Methodist Church, these are most visible in the United States. Small groups are available for women, men, singles, youths, and retirees. The groups can run for years. Others are much more ad hoc, coming together for a period, serving their purpose, and then ceasing to exist. Yet others have been inaugurated more formally as programmes.

Two of these programmes deserve mention: Disciple Bible Study and Christian Believer. The first Disciple Bible Study involves an intensive thirty-four-week study in small groups that takes the student through the whole Bible. Later versions pick up various books of the Bible. The studies are led by lay workers, involve the use of videos, and are remarkably ambitious in terms of student commitment required. Some have been made available in languages other than English. Christian Believer, using a similar format, takes up issues of theology, but has been too highbrow and thus unsuccessful. In addition a variety of studies developed by well-known local preachers like Adam Hamilton have become extremely popular.

One other effective small group operation is known as The Walk to Emmaus. This began as a weekend retreat in Spain in the Roman Catholic Church where seekers were given an intensive course in Christian initiation. It was known as 'Cursillo'. United Methodists picked it up, got permission to change the name and adapt it, and systematically introduced it across the denomination. The preparation for the retreats is both labour and cost intensive. The results have been startling in terms of introducing Methodists to the core ideas of prevenient, justifying, and sanctifying grace. Many have come to experience the kind of deep assurance that was once a hallmark of Methodism but which has become marginal in many church circles. Following the retreat, those who attend are encouraged to become members of small Emmaus groups that help them work through their experiences. Members are also invited to attend a final climactic service of the Lord's Supper where they can revisit their own experience and recommit to Christian discipleship. The Emmaus Movement, as it is now known, has been exported to other parts of Methodism outside the United States of America.

On a smaller scale a final development is now beginning to fire the imagination. Elaine Heath, a scholar of mysticism, has initiated a movement known as New Monasticism which began within United Methodism in Dallas but has reached across denominational and national boundaries. The core of the movement centres on establishing monastic houses within poor neighbourhoods where Christians gather together to form units of intentional discipleship to serve the poor. There is an important postmodern orientation at play in the movement in which various practices from the great monastic traditions are picked up and implemented. There is enormous emphasis on learning the art of prayer and spiritual direction. The dream in part is to bring about a whole reorientation not just in the life of the church but in the formation of theological students and in the very nature of theology itself. Heath has recently become the Dean of Duke Divinity School, one of the elite theological schools of United Methodism, and has earned the accolade of pioneer in new forms of spirituality and ministry. Only time will tell if this version of new monasticism can survive the temptations of theological faddishness and relativism. I am sure that other forms of monasticism which are more intentionally rooted in the monastic traditions of East and West will be invented. I know of at least one that is currently under construction.

Many Methodists look back at the early days and yearn for a return to the prudential practices that were so effective in forming Christians. However, where these have been long abandoned, they cannot be placed in the microwave and reheated for contemporary consumption. The classical means of grace represented by baptism and the Lord's Supper, the study of scripture, and prayer will always have their place in Methodism. The search to replace the functional equivalents of the ad hoc means of grace invented in the first generation has been intense across the years. Many of the ensuing experiments have proved to be remarkably successful. The difficulty in the present situation is that there is no theological consensus on what to teach and what to do in order to make disciples who make a real difference in the world. This is inevitable given the pluralism that was implanted in United Methodism in 1972 but which has been challenged on several fronts in recent years. The situation is chaotic; yet the freedom involved in chaos can often lead to important discoveries and innovations.

One important rediscovery has emerged out of the recent discussion on means of grace. Originally, Christians spoke of works of piety and works of mercy. The former were simply various spiritual practices that mediated divine grace; the latter were various human actions directed at helping others. Now works of mercy, following an insight by Wesley, have come to be seen as an important means of grace. Thus in, say, trying to help the poor, we may find it a work that is far beyond us in terms of the demands laid on us. As a result, it can force us back to draw on the energy and wisdom of God, finding this essential in sustaining effective action. This simple transposition of works of mercy has been important in propelling Methodists out into society and the world at large in order to make a difference.

Chapter 7
The impact of Methodism

Social holiness

The Methodist commitment to holiness is both personal and social. Personal holiness is the individual's reorientation from sinners to saints through the manifold grace of God. Personal holiness depends crucially on social practices, or social holiness. These practices are the classical means of grace represented by baptism and the Lord's Supper, supplemented by prudential means of grace from class meetings to Bible studies. Hence Methodists have been devoted to going to meetings; membership initially in a Methodist society and later in a Methodist church has been a sacred duty. However, over time social holiness took on an extended meaning. Genuine personal holiness is expressed in love for God and neighbour. Love for neighbour is not some kind of insubstantial, abstract emotion; it is expressed in personal and corporate action in society and history. As such, Methodists have opposed any and every form of dead orthodoxy; they want a living orthodoxy that transforms the world. They want a social holiness that fixes society.

The transition from personal holiness to social holiness in this second sense is neither smooth nor error-free. Both forms of holiness can readily go off the rails. Both can readily morph into suffocating moralism. Both can involve serious errors in moral discernment, cultivating various forms of self-deception. In the case of social holiness there is the additional possibility of being seriously mistaken about how to fix the ills of society. Make a mistake on the causes and you will also make a mistake on the solutions.

Negative assessments

The Marxist historian, Edward P. Thompson, has suggested that Methodism was a distraction that led the working class to focus on heaven and on illusory spiritual goods rather than on tackling the genuine problems of poverty and class that arose with the Industrial Revolution. This was in part a response to the thesis of Élie Halévy that claimed that Methodism saved England from the kind of bloody revolution that happened in France. Interestingly, in the early 19th century the British government considered shutting down Methodism. They feared that it harboured exactly the kind of revolutionary fervour that had rocked France. Methodists in high places prevented this from happening. Not surprisingly, it was in this period that Jabez Bunting, who tried to rule British Methodism with an iron hand, insisted that Methodists should hate democracy as much as they hate sin.

On a very different level critics have worried that Methodism was a form of repressed eroticism that was dangerous for healthy human development. The intense forms of experience of the divine—sometimes couched in sensual imagery of intercourse with the divine or marriage to the Saviour—lent support to this interpretation of the impact of Methodism. Folk worried in parts of Cornwall that Methodist love feasts were covers for orgies.

It is hard to take the latter interpretation of Methodism seriously. It looks upon human action merely from a third-person perspective as an outsider and ignores the crucial place of first-person perspectives on human action. However, it highlights one reason why I have chosen the term 'impact' to cover the material of this chapter. 'Impact' is a relatively neutral term that keeps open whether the impact was good, bad, mixed, or indifferent. It also signals that the evidence presented is contested.

It is clear that the initial impact of Methodism upon the Church of England is a very mixed story. The Wesley brothers died as members but most of their followers left the latter; any leavening of the parent body was interrupted. Methodists went their own way and took their virtues and vices with them. However, there is no doubt that Methodism influenced most branches of Evangelicalism inside and outside the Anglican tradition. Its Arminian theology gave encouragement to evangelism; its stress on holiness gave a boost to homegrown holiness movements; and the hymns of Charles Wesley permeated the practices of worship and of devotion.

Saints galore

When we turn to Methodism as an independent operation, we begin by noting that Methodism has produced its fair share of saints. John Fletcher and his wife Mary Bosanquet (1739–1815) were readily acknowledged as such in the early days. As vicar of a poor parish, Fletcher was once asked by government officials what reward would be appropriate given that he had made comments that were helpful to the government of the day. He did not know how to answer and eventually said all he ever wanted was to become more holy. Mary Bosanquet was a careful student of mysticism and a deaconess known for her deep spirituality. She described her life grandly as walking on the highway of holiness and as longing for a mind fixed on all the silent heaven of love. Take a later example, that of Gordon Wilson (1927–95), an Irish Methodist who was a well-known local shopkeeper from Enniskillen. His daughter, Marie, was among eleven innocent civilians killed in an IRA terrorist attack on the town on 8 November 1987. Gordon himself was injured. That Sunday afternoon he came on television and insisted that there be no revenge killings in response to the terrible events of the morning. He was later appointed to the Irish Senate in Dublin and worked valiantly for the peace process that was eventually brokered on Good Friday, 20 April 1998. These are just three of a host of folk who have exhibited conspicuous sanctity across the years. Many of their names show up on the list of recipients of the World Methodist Peace Prize.

The impact on social movements

Shifting to look at social movements that were deeply influenced by Methodism, the obvious examples are that of the abolition of slavery in the 19th century and the Temperance Movement in the 20th.

Opposition to slavery goes right back to John Wesley himself. He wrote a hard-hitting piece called 'Thoughts Upon Slavery' as early as 1774. He confronted his readers with the brutal realities involved, insisted that slavery was irreconcilable with justice, mercy, and the love of God, and found slaveholders guilty of 'frauds, robberies, and murders'. This radical position was initially adopted by the Methodist Episcopal Church. However, the church split in 1844. The presenting issue was the fact that a bishop in the South had inherited slaves through marriage. When he refused to liberate them the matter became a dividing issue at the General Conference. However, much more was at stake than the behaviour of a single bishop; massive economic and racial factors came into play which could not be contained within the body as a whole. Many of the abolitionists were old-style Methodists committed to the practices of revival. Some of them were expelled from the church and founded their own denominations. The Wesleyan Church and the Free Methodist Church trace their origins back to this sorry episode in the history of Methodism. The 'Free' in Free Methodism meant free rather than rented pews, freedom from secret societies, freedom rather than formality in worship, and freedom for slaves.

Methodists were also heavily involved in the Temperance Movement which sought either the regulation of the sale of alcoholic beverages or its total abolition. To this day Methodists can be nervous about alcohol, a corporate disposition that arose because of a long-lasting battle with the problem of drunkenness. Most official Methodist meetings will not serve alcoholic drinks. The opposition was initially directed against hard liquor and then extended to include all alcohol. By 1830 the average American over 15 years of age consumed close to seven gallons of pure alcohol a year. Because of total opposition to alcohol, 'temperance' really meant teetotalism. Albert Outler once quipped that many Methodists were committed to teetotal depravity in their doctrine of sin. Given the opposition to the abuse of alcohol it is no surprise that Methodists were heavily opposed to the drinking of alcohol. This was the case in both Britain and North America. In the latter case, the movement took up the radical stance of prohibiting the sale of alcohol. Many of the foot soldiers and leaders of the movement were Methodists, like Frances Willard (1839–98), some of whom saw their crusade as part of their wider progressive agenda that included the abolition of slavery. In the end the movement failed as a political project. Its influence bore fruit in the formation of the Salvation Army, a radical off-shoot of Methodism that abandoned the Lord's Supper because of its ministry to those addicted to alcohol. The mother church found a solution when Thomas Bramwell Welch emigrated from England to the United States and invented Welch's grape juice, which he sold as unfermented wine. It has been widely used within North American Methodism.

Politics proper

The place of Methodism in politics proper is an ambiguous one. John Wesley was an English Tory in the tradition of Edmund Burke. He was deeply committed to the organic integration of monarchy, church, and parliament. He was effectively a public moralist who looked to relatively small-scale change and to voluntary associations to bring about social and political reform. Yet he sowed seeds that could readily be taken in a more radical direction once they were let loose in the world. Thus the whole drive to seek radical personal sanctity could readily be transformed into a drive to seek radical social change. There were utopian elements waiting to be exploited. In some cases Methodist preaching directed at personal liberation could be interpreted with an additional layer of meaning directed to social liberation. Thus preaching that used the exodus from Egypt as an analogy for personal salvation could also be heard by slaves as a message of hope for emancipation and a word of assurance that such hope could become a reality. This happened even when the preacher's intention was the opposite; they were expecting conversion to generate a passive attitude to the existing social order.

We can see here a radical element in Methodism that showed up most conspicuously in the role of Methodism in the creation of the Labour Movement that led to the forming of the Labour Party in England. Eric Hobsbawm, a Marxist historian, challenged the claims of Edward P. Thompson noted earlier, and wrote of the Primitive Methodists that '... it is not too much to think of them as primarily a sect of trade union cadres'. Other historians—W. R. Ward, Alan Gilbert, David Hempton, Hugh MacLeod, and Nigel Scotland—have also highlighted the role of Methodists in 19th-century movements for social reform. Much of the leadership of establishment Methodism was conservative and reactionary. However, they could not suppress the drive at the grass roots level to work for a new day for the poor and the working class. Six of the seven Tolpuddle Martyrs were Methodists and were led by a Methodist local preacher, George Loveless. The Tolpuddle Martyrs were a group of Dorset farm workers who were arrested and convicted of swearing a secret oath as members of the Friendly Society of Agricultural Workers. In 1837 they were sentenced to penal transportation to Australia. Subsequently they were pardoned after mass protests on their behalf. They became heroes to many who were committed to improving the conditions of the working class in England.

Beyond this dramatic example, Methodists show up in a network of labour organizations like cooperative shops and trade unions. In Russia, there is the remarkable case of Julius Hecker (1881–1938) who became a communist who retained his Methodist faith, and who, despite his loyalty to the state, was executed by Stalin. Hecker deployed the lessons he learned from the teaching of pastors during his studies in the United States to the education of workers back home in Russia. He also developed a brand of porridge that is still sold in stores in Moscow.

Why was this the case? There are a raft of reasons: Methodists inherited a tradition of protest from Wesley against local clergy and rich landlords; they were taught to read in Methodist Sunday schools; they were given the linguistic tools to speak their mind in class meetings; they were drawn into the local leadership of Methodist societies where they picked up management skills; they learned to speak in public when they became local preachers; they drew on the national three-tiered organization of local society, district, and Annual Conference and transferred it to their reform organizations; they used their experience in organizing camp meetings to hold mass meetings; they drew on simple methods of collecting money and applied it to providing funding to workers on strike so that the latter could succeed in their goals; and they were strongly energized by the spirituality and piety of Methodism which had a strong egalitarian streak in its foundations.

Some Methodists like Hugh Price Hughes (1847–1902) in the 19th century and Lord Soper (1903–98) in the 20th century became committed socialists. These commanded national audiences for their political ideas. Hughes was a towering figure in his day, producing his own newspaper, *The Methodist Times*, to propagate his own brand of socialism. Soper was a brilliant open-air speaker in Hyde Park in London; a beloved minister in a London City Mission which reached out to the poor; a first-rate broadcaster; and a Labour member of the House of Lords.

Think and let think

While some radical Methodists were more than ready to identify the Gospel with the arrival of socialism, this was never a majority opinion within Methodism. One reason for this is that the Methodist tradition has from the beginning encouraged diversity of judgement in the political arena. This stems in part from the Methodist vision of authority and reason. Just as the New Testament does not mandate any specific polity for the organization of church life, so there is no blueprint for the organization of our social and political life. We are not given special revelation in this arena; we are to rely on reason and experience. Methodists are to think and to let think. As a result, when it comes to the use of lethal force, Methodists have been committed to both pacifism and just war theory. Both options can be found in the *Book of Discipline* of the United Methodist Church. Two of the leading moral theologians in contemporary Methodism make visible the diversity: Stanley Hauerwas is a pacifist; Robin Lovin is a realist. Equally illuminating, Methodists can be found on both the conservative and progressive wings of politics. In North American politics they are represented by George W. Bush and Hillary Clinton. Bush, after his conversion, was deeply influenced by his membership in a moderate version of Methodism in Texas; he was very interested in voluntary, faith-based organizations in dealing with social problems. Clinton was radicalized through her youth group in Methodist circles in Chicago; she wrote a thesis on the radical politics of Saul Alinsky (1909–72), an influential community organizer and radical politician; and she is clearly committed to the state as the primary agent in dealing with social challenges.

The diversity can be further exemplified on the ground by looking at Methodism in Africa. One example will suffice. When the slave trade was abolished, the British government decided to establish a 'Province of Freedom' in late 1787. The province became Sierra Leone. Some of the 'Black Poor' of London were persuaded to go to Sierra Leone where the plan was to develop a flourishing agricultural society free of slaves and free of a governor. Around the same time some of the black Americans who had fought on the British side in the American Revolutionary War, and who had been resettled in Nova Scotia, expressed interest in relocating to Sierra Leone. The Methodists who moved to Sierra Leone brought with them competing views of the relation between the church and state. The Methodists from England brought with them an integrated vision of church and state; they desired to support and be supported by the government. The Methodists from Nova Scotia brought with them, as one of their critics put it, 'the American Republican spirit and are averse to government'. They wanted the separation of church and state.

Impact on education

One of the most important expressions of social holiness in Methodism shows up in its role in education. Begin with a prosaic example. There are around 50,000 Methodists in Ireland, yet they have built two outstanding grammar schools—Wesley College in Dublin and Methodist College in Belfast—and an agricultural college in Gurteen in the Republic of Ireland. The pattern of building excellent grammar schools can be found in British Methodism and throughout the world. These schools have been critical to the education of a network of students who went on to play a prominent role in politics after Britain systematically abandoned its colonial ambitions.

Colonial leaders were far from always being happy with the role that missionaries played in their schools. It was not that the missionaries were intentionally subversive. Education, along with the provision of healthcare, was simply a natural way of serving the people they had come to convert. However, the effects of the education led students to challenge the status quo and prepared them to govern.

It is often thought that missionaries were simply agents of colonial power. There is truth in this claim, for missionaries inevitably brought with them their own imperial and paternalistic ways of thinking. However, the reality was much more complex. Nelson Mandela captures what was at issue:

> Yet even with such attitudes, I believe their benefits outweighed their disadvantages. The missionaries ran schools when the government was unwilling or unable to do so. The learning environment of the missionary schools, while often rigid, was far more open that the racist principles underlying government schools.

Lammen Sanneh, a leading historian of mission, goes further and argues that the missionaries played a significant role in preserving the cultures of the native peoples of Africa. By translating the scriptures into the native languages, they preserved the languages and thereby preserved precious elements in the host culture. This in turn provided the platform for the explosion of independent African churches after colonial rule ended.

The role of education by Methodists in the United States of America took off in a different direction. Methodists decided that they should devote their energies to the state system at the primary and secondary level; this was a way to serve the culture as a whole rather than withdrawing into their own private school system. However, they enthusiastically gave themselves and their money to the building of colleges and universities across the continent. There are currently no less than 119 schools, universities, and colleges that are recognized by the University Senate of the United Methodist Church, the body responsible for their oversight. One of the member schools is Southern Methodist University, in Dallas, Texas, which is fully owned by the United Methodist Church. It has just celebrated its centenary and raised over $1 billion for future developments. Other top-flight universities have become independent, flourishing as private institutions. The list includes Northwestern, Syracuse, the University of Southern California, and Vanderbilt. In 1991, Africa University in Mutare, Zimbabwe, was founded by the African bishops of the United

Methodist Church and is going from strength to strength. In
Liberia the African Methodist Episcopal University was established
in Monrovia in 1995 and has over 3,000 students. Beyond this,
even the smaller Methodist bodies have founded their own
universities. Seattle Pacific University in Seattle, Washington, is
a splendid liberal arts institution that was established by the
Free Methodist Church and has just recently added a seminary.
Indiana Wesleyan University in Marion, Indiana, was founded
by the Wesleyan Church and has become a model of extension or
distance education throughout the state of Indiana.

One of the crucial challenges facing the larger Methodist
universities, especially those that are full research institutions, is
how to maintain any kind of Methodist footprint in the curriculum
and in the university as a whole. Methodists have long been
champions of academic freedom. They recognize that a great
university will have scholars from many faith traditions and none.
The challenge of integrating their faith-based heritage into the
life of the university is now being raised in fresh and constructive
ways. Hence there has been a marked tendency to allow the
universities to follow their own agenda, so long as space is available
for the office of chaplain or for a school of theology where that
applies. Colleges and universities from more conservative
Methodist denominations have been more successful in this
arena. However, they have not yet been able to move to the
more ambitious goal of the research-based university.

Methodist hospitals

In terms of the Methodist contribution to education, there stands
close by the contribution of Methodism to health systems and
hospitals. One extraordinary example that will serve our purpose
here can be found in the Houston Methodist Medical Center in
Houston, Texas (Figure 7). Aside from its work as a general
hospital, 'Houston Methodist' has become a leading medical
research centre with six community hospitals in the Houston area.

7. **Methodist Medical Center in Houston, Texas.**

The research centre is led by a team of international specialists; the director is a brilliant polymath with a deep Catholic faith; it has magnificent facilities for its work; it has an astonishing endowment; the chaplain is a spiritual visionary; and it has developed a set of core values that are derived from the Methodist heritage. There are currently exploratory talks with Perkins School of Theology at Southern Methodist University, looking at ways in which theologians, medical researchers, and practitioners might enrich each other's work. All this is done in a spirit of intellectual freedom and rigorous intellectual engagement.

John Wesley in his own inimitable way took a deep interest in the medical practices of his day. He left Oxford to give himself to a small renewal movement made of a loyal band of young enthusiasts in search of holiness. In a *Short Account* of the school he established at Kingswood he included a diatribe against the Oxford system. Henry Rack summarizes his complaints as follows:

> The professorial lectures are useless; many of the tutors lack learning and religion; the public 'exercises' and 'disputations'

91

for degrees are 'an idle, useless interruption of any useful studies' and 'shockingly superficial'. Socially a man gains all kinds of 'company' 'except that which would do him good'. The prospect of holy orders as the reward of the system is nothing compared with eternity.

In leaving and criticizing his alma mater he was not rejecting education, he was reaching for a better vision of education. Moreover, he was insisting that an interest in education must never override the privileged place of eternity in our lives.

The wider cultural scene

One wonders what John Wesley would make of the extraordinary impact of Methodism across the years. There is much to ponder. And I have not touched on the impact of Methodism on either popular culture or high culture. In the former I think of Willie Nelson learning to sing gospel songs in his local Methodist church in Abbot, Texas. When the church in Abbot was closed, Nelson and a friend purchased the property so that services could continue. Nearby is the town of Lukenbach, Texas, a place of pilgrimage for devotees of country music. Nelson returns annually for the Fourth of July picnic with thousands of his friends. The place was made famous in one of his songs that sounds like a secular version of love in Methodism.

> The only two things in life that make it worth livin'
> Is guitars tuned good and firm-feelin' women;
> I don't need my name in the marquee lights;
> I got my songs and I got you with me tonight.
> Maybe it's time we got back to the basics of love.

As to high culture, one would have to spend time in Boston Avenue United Methodist Church, one of the great architectural wonders of Tulsa, Oklahoma, that was built in 1927–9 at a cost of $1.5 million. The building occupies a whole city block, has 200 rooms, and has a 280 feet high tower. Over the south porch there is a statue of Jesus, flanked by statues of Francis Asbury and John Wesley. I suspect these kinds of developments would keep Wesley awake at night, worrying. So too would the decline that stalks Methodism in Britain and North America.

Chapter 8
The decline of Methodism

Keeping count

From the beginning, with John Wesley in the lead, Methodists have been very fussy about numbers. Numbers mattered because people mattered; statistics kept track of people who needed and found salvation. And numbers provided data for analysing what was going on and for making informed decisions about strategies for extending the spread of the gospel. Wesley's comments are ad hoc and unsystematic but they have imprinted on Methodists a keen eye for numerical records that remains intact to this day. Yet he was not merely interested in numbers; he was also interested in quality control. Thus decline was never merely a matter of numbers, it was also a matter of decline in the overarching mission of Methodism to cultivate conspicuous sanctity.

Speaking to his lay preachers, he wrote:

> Observe: It is not your business to preach so many times, and to take care of this or that society; but to save as many souls as you can; to bring as many sinners as you possibly can to repentance and with all your power to build them up into that holiness without which they cannot see the Lord.

In 1786, he began a review of the landscape of Methodism with a warning:

> I am not afraid that the people called Methodists should ever cease to exist in Europe or America. But I am afraid lest they should only exist as a dead sect, having the form of religion without the power. And this undoubtedly will be the case unless they hold fast both the doctrine, spirit, and discipline with which they first set out.

The statistics

The issue of numerical decline has become something of an obsession with Methodists in Europe and the United States. Let's begin with the situation in Britain. A report, *Statistics in Mission*, issued in 2014 tracked the decline over a ten-year period. In 2003 there were 304,971 members; in 2013 there were 208,738 members. This represented a 3.7 per cent year-on-year decline and a reduction of 29.35 per cent overall. Children's attendance fell from 77,900 in 2003 to 32,700 in 2013, a reduction of 58 per cent.

This decline is part of the wider decline of Christianity in the Anglo-Saxon and Celtic world. Church of England numbers fell from 40 per cent of the population in 1983 to 29 per cent in 2004 to 17 per cent in 2014. British Roman Catholic numbers fell from 10 to 8 per cent between 1983 and 2014, a figure that masks the arrival of Catholic immigrants. The membership of the Church of Scotland has fallen off the cliff: from 36 per cent in 2001 to 18 per cent in 2013. Extend the numbers across Europe in terms of church attendance and the situation is even bleaker. In Britain, 1.4 per cent attend church weekly, in France 1.2 per cent, and in Germany 0.9 per cent.

The statistics for Methodist decline in the United States are not as bad as in Europe, but they tell a similar story. In 1968, the United

Methodist Church in the United States had 11,026,976 members; in 2012 the number was 7,391,911; this was a decline of 33 per cent.

Let's dig in and look at an example. Methodism began in New York, brought there by Irish Methodists who founded John Street Methodist Church in what is now the financial district of Manhattan on 12 October 1766. By the early 1800s the New York area was identified by the Methodist historian, Abel Stevens, as 'the garden of Methodism'. New York was home to Phoebe Palmer, the crucial leader in the renewal of Methodism known as the 'Holiness Movement', in the middle of the 19th century. In 2006, there were 124,000 United Methodists in the New York Conference, an area with a population of twenty million. Today the membership of the conference has fallen to under 100,000, a decline of 19.35 per cent. Worship attendance has fallen from 38,000 in 2006 to 30,000 in 2015, or a decline of 21 per cent in nine years.

These statistics fit with the wider picture in mainline Protestant churches. In 1966, the Episcopal Church had 3,647,297 members; in 2013 it had 1,866,758 members—a decline of 49 per cent. The Presbyterian Church in the USA had 3,304,321 members in 1967; in 2013 it had 1,760,200, a decline of 47 per cent. In 1987, the Evangelical Lutheran Church in America had 5,288,230 members; in 2013 it had 3,863,133—a decline of 27 per cent.

Megatheories of decline

The search for reasons for the decline of Methodism in Britain and North America is a cottage industry in itself. The most popular cause of decline until recently has been tied to a story of secularization in the West as whole.

Leading social theorists have argued that crucial intellectual and social trends in the modern period rendered all religion essentially obsolete. The argument is cumulative. The rise of science and the mode of rationality that made it so successful undermined confidence in divine revelation. As more democratic states emerged, the authority of the church was diminished in the public arena. Domains previously dominated by the church, such as charitable organizations, education, and medical care, were taken over by the state. The rise of state governments produced bureaucracies which appealed to generic rational considerations like happiness, fairness, and equality that ignored theological considerations. As the industrial revolution took hold, the church found itself marooned in villages and rural settings, while the masses flooded the cities; the churches had no strategy for ministering to their needs.

Over time Christendom—the marriage of throne, church, and parliament—crumbled. The Christian faith was pushed to the margins of society; it became an entirely private affair and thus lost the props that had held it in place for centuries. The process of secularization really took off in Britain in the 1960s, but the seeds were sown centuries before. The decline of Methodism, on this view, simply reflects the inexorable laws of social change as applied to Europe from the 18th century onwards.

Another explanation focuses more on intellectual changes in British culture. The story in this case picks up on the rise of science and argues that science means an end to all claims to divine intervention or miracle in the world. More dramatically it undermines the standard story of a six-day creation that had long been central to Christianity. Theories of cosmology and evolution showed Christian theological claims about nature and about human origins to be false. Historical investigation followed in the wake of science by looking for purely natural and human causes for historical events. When applied to the Bible it undercuts the whole raft of miracle stories, including the incarnation of the Son of God in Jesus Christ. Philosophy in the wake of David Hume and Immanuel Kant developed the theoretical consequences of these developments at the highest levels of European culture.

Sociologists for their part began to provide entirely naturalistic accounts of the origins of religion that had nothing to do with providence or the hand of God. Hence traditional Christian claims became no longer credible. The whole Christian story of creation–fall–redemption thus fell apart rationally.

Theologians tried valiantly to face the new intellectual challenges that emerged but there was no agreement on what to do. Some lost their nerve and sought to strike a bargain with the new knowledge; the life of these bargains turned out to be in the region of thirty years. Others dug in and became reactionary, inventing a fundamentalist version of Christianity that clung to the Bible as the ultimate truth about everything and waged a rearguard war on modernity at the margins of society. Others tried to develop ways to try to keep as much of the old faith as possible, seeking to translate the gospel into the language of today's culture and thereby keep it relevant.

Critics of Christianity represented by forms of militant atheism saw these various reactions as last-ditch efforts to save a lost cause. In my student years at university, I encountered striking examples of the 'old atheism' in full swing at that time. The general attitude to religion was one of benign neglect. Critics were tolerant of religion, for it gave comfort to many people: religion is often a useful cultural glue that holds things together—it was thought not to be a good idea to scare the horses, as it were, and to let the common folk have their religion, for who knew what they would do without it. Many of the 'old atheists' were buried with full religious honours as Jews or Christians. The later more militant forms of atheism, represented by Richard Dawkins, Christopher Hitchens, Daniel Dennett, and Sam Harris, have had no time for this kind of benign neglect; religion is a poison or disease that needs to be eradicated.

On this theory of decline, Methodism is simply one more casualty among others.

Both of these explanations have been exported to the United States in order to explain the decline of United Methodism. The first—the secular theory—can only travel so far. It ignores significant differences between Europe and the United States. In fact, David Martin has argued for decades that the theory is undermined by what has happened there. The full forces of modernity have been unleashed in the United States but this has been accompanied by the flourishing of Christian denominations. What became a nominally secular state let loose the various Christian denominations to compete with one another; this competition proved to be exceptionally fruitful in its effects. Methodism was well-placed to take full advantage of this situation, and not surprisingly it became the largest Protestant denomination in the United States in the 19th century. Moreover, its democratic ethos and pragmatism fitted nicely with the needs of the New World. So the application of the model to explain decline in Britain does not work for the United States. More generally, the story of secularization may indeed only apply to Europe. Religions are flourishing elsewhere. In China we cannot keep up with the numbers of Christians as the church there is growing so fast. Social theorists were projecting their own loss of faith and their own hopes for the future onto the national and cosmic landscape.

The second theory—the change in the intellectual scenery and the subsequent loss of nerve in accommodation to secular culture—has been more favourably received as an explanation for the decline of United Methodism. The story is simple: progressive and liberal churches decline; conservative and evangelical churches survive and grow. The claim is repeated again and again in conservative United Methodist circles. On this view, the hallmark of liberal and progressive churches is that they do not believe the Bible. The crucial issue is the loss of authority. Once churches lose the authority of the Bible then they are cast on a sea of relativism where anything goes, theologically and morally. Churches can then no longer convert outsiders or a new generation; nor can they keep the serious Christians who head for the door and go to the neighbourhood evangelical church or journey on to full unbelief. Many think that this is essentially the story of mainline Protestantism in the United States; and Methodism, as a 'mainline' Protestant denomination, fits this pattern. The statistics I gave earlier readily secure this conclusion. Or so some scholars think.

In Britain, the response to the challenge of decline has focused on adopting various strategies of change that might turn things around. This has dovetailed with an independent desire to return to the Church of England with the hope of finding a new lease of life for the future. Many Methodists who identify as evangelical in a broad sense, while not necessarily opposed to this, fear the loss of the distinctive identity and gifts of the tradition.

In the United States, while the commitment to church unity is built into the very constitution of the church, the drive towards church unity is no longer a priority. There has been a concerted effort to tackle the challenge of decline head-on, although there is no consensus on how to do this. The major problem is one of survival.

The General Conference of 1984 voted late at night to set a goal of twenty million members by 1992. In 1986, Bishop Richard B. Wilke followed up with a short book, *And Are We Yet Alive*, which became a manifesto for the drive to deploy the resources of the Church Growth Movement to achieve this illusory goal. Wilke himself knew that the goal was illusory. However, he soldiered on in hope. George Hunter III, a leading expert in church growth studies, kept the goal alive in a series of books and workshops that changed pockets of the culture of United Methodism from pessimism to optimistic pragmatism. Millions of dollars were spent on church growth seminars across the church. Later, millions were spent on an advertising campaign with the slogan, 'Open hearts. Open minds. Open doors'. The slogan continues to be used to this day.

Conservatives naturally think the solution is to return to the authority of the Bible, retrieve the classical doctrines of Methodism, and get serious about evangelism. Much of the energy is given to fending off the agenda of their progressive colleagues, especially as this relates to such hot-button issues as abortion and homosexuality. Within this there is a yearning for a fresh outpouring of the Holy Spirit in a third Great Awakening. Albert Outler responded to this yearning with an inimitable quip: there will be no third Great Awakening until we realize that the second one is over. He also once remarked that United Methodists are as united as Free Methodists are free, a quip that could more specifically be applied to the network of conservatives and evangelicals. There is less agreement among them than their progressive critics fear.

A very different agenda has emerged out of the conservative wing of the church, and gained traction beyond, that sees the problem of decline in terms drawn from the tradition of monastic spirituality. The pioneer leader in this case is Elaine Heath. She trained as a systematic theologian, switched to the study of evangelism, and over ten years has established a version of new monasticism that is spreading worldwide. As noted earlier, she and her cohorts represent a whole new renewal movement within United Methodism. The heart of the response is to tackle the dark night of the soul that bedevils North American Christianity by establishing small communities rooted in the ancient spiritual practices of the church, and directed to the care of creation, social justice, and deep conversion.

Progressives within United Methodism look to a very different solution than the one provided in the main by conservatives. They want United Methodism to find up-to-date ways to express the faith for a new generation. They propose that the church further its inclusivist agenda by changing its position on homosexual marriage and on the ordination of gay and lesbian candidates for ministry. They seek greater assertiveness in the problems of racism, poverty, and immigration. They believe United Methodism should find whole new ways to think about evangelism rather than recovering older practices that no longer work. They want United Methodist schools of theology to commit to liberation theology and further that agenda by exploring and rooting out all forms of oppression and marginalization.

This latter agenda is especially lifted up by a more radical wing of the progressive side of the church. John J. Vincent in England and Joerg Rieger in the United States propose that the vision of the church as a whole 'is best shaped and transformed not from the top down but from the bottom up, by perspectives from the margins'. United Methodists, with other Christians, should dig down into the roots of contemporary life. This means finding out the real causes of poverty and oppression, and joining in God's mission of liberation in the world. Yet the truth about God's action in the world cannot be found without getting involved in grassroots communities who refuse to compromise their faith in the living God. The result entails intentional opposition to both conservative and centrist groups that identify their sectional social and political interests with some kind of bogus common interest. In the light of this proposal, the obsession with decline is really a distraction. United Methodists should focus on divine action in history and leave the outcome to God.

Another group, deeply influenced by Stanley Hauerwas and William H. Willimon (two exceptionally influential scholars who taught for years at Duke University), suggests that United Methodism should adopt the stance of resident aliens and abandon its traditional, cosy relation with North American nationalism and capitalism. God is effectively killing the United Methodist Church because of its compromises with American culture. It should boldly reject this relationship, openly owning a sectarian stance against it, rather than pretend that it can transform that culture. What is needed is a recovery of nerve with respect to the truth of the gospel, a new trust in divine power transmitted through the sacraments, and a fresh confidence in the church as a colony of heaven. They are especially tired of the niceness exhibited by United Methodist clergy.

> ...the church is dying a slow death at the hands of pastors who are nice, pastors who are themselves miserable because they are attempting to 'help people' with no basis for that help, and no safeguard for themselves, other than their desire to be nice and help people. Indeed, one of us is tempted to think that there is not much wrong with the church that could not be cured by God calling about a hundred really insensitive, uncaring, and offensive people into the ministry.

Reviewing the numbers

Ted A. Campbell, a United Methodist historian, has taken a very different approach in the debate about decline. He has challenged the thesis at its foundations. He agrees that United Methodism is a mainline Protestant denomination in the United States but pushes back into the history to challenge the significance of the statistics cited above. The statistics are accurate; but, as we all know, statistics have to be carefully interpreted. Campbell also agrees that United Methodism belongs on the liberal and progressive side of the division in American Christianity. Why does he reject the popular theory that the cause of decline is to be found in the abandoning of a conservative theology? Here is what he argues. Once you go back and take a longer track of statistics the historic Protestant churches were never the dominant centre of American religion. They never accounted for more than 16.8 per cent of the US population from 1925 to 2000. Overall worship attendance in all religious groups (not just historic churches) has declined since 2000. Weekly church attendance figures in historic Protestant churches have declined at a slower rate than overall membership figures, suggesting that the majority losses have been of inactive members. Those who actually participate in their churches are a stronger percentage of membership than they were forty years ago. There is a strong core of believers in the historic churches, despite all the claims that have been made to the contrary. While Protestant churches have tolerated liberal views among members and leaders, the official doctrines and liturgies remained traditional and orthodox in content. The progressive social activism of the historic churches, for example, in the civil rights movement was not a rejection of the gospel; it was grounded in the gospel. The statistics from the newer evangelical churches show that their gains seldom come from members of the historic churches; and there are 'defections' both ways.

Applied to United Methodism, what is really happening is that they are losing nominal members. Given that Wesley was interested in real Christians rather than nominal Christians, United Methodist should not heed the popular exaggerations that flood the airwaves.

Positive results

I think there is some truth in Campbell's analysis, but even he has to acknowledge the stark truths about decline. United Methodists have in fact heeded the challenge represented by stories of decline and are seeking to address it. They have adopted a new mission statement focused on the making of disciples. They have shown enormous flexibility in worship, reaching out to a new generation in the idioms and forms that connect with them. Bishops have appointed younger pastors more quickly to larger congregations than has been the custom in order to connect better with young families. Seminaries have appointed professors of evangelism to renew this vital ministry of outreach and to provide intellectual resources for best practices. Annual Conferences and other agencies have established think-tanks to tackle the challenge of decline and to implement effective change. As a result it is no accident that there is a network of United Methodist megachurches, some of which have become flagship examples of renewal. Some of them function like mini-denominations which launch all sorts of service projects, locally and internationally; they also establish healthy daughter churches that are thriving. All of them share a preferential option for the poor in their ministries, working for and with the poor as best they can.

Wesley's diagnosis

As I noted at the outset, John Wesley was worried about the future of the Methodists. In 1789, he was so distressed that he turned his despair about their future into a problem of cosmic proportions. Wesley was gripped by a sense that Christianity had failed to make good on its promise to save the world. He takes an imaginary tour around the world starting with the 'heathens', pausing with the various Christian denominations, and ending with Methodism. He finds no solace in what he perceives. He gives close attention to the Methodists. The deep cause of failure there is the absence of self-denial. More to the point, the failure stemmed from the failure to heed his advice on money: 'to make all you can, save all you can, and give all you can'. He ponders the possibility of having imposed a dress code akin to that of the Quakers. 'But alas! The time is now past. And what I can do now I cannot tell.' His conclusion is so famous that it is known as Wesley's law.

> Does this not seem (and yet this it cannot be!) that Christianity, true scriptural Christianity, has a tendency in process of time to undermine and destroy itself? For wherever true Christianity spreads it must cause diligence and frugality, which, in the natural course of things, must beget riches. And riches naturally beget pride, love of the world, and every temper that is destructive of Christianity. Now if there be no way to prevent this, Christianity is consistent with itself, and, of consequence, cannot stand, cannot continue; since, wherever it prevails, it saps its own foundation.

His only solution—offered without much confidence—is to reiterate his admonition to make all you can, save all you can, and give all you can. Wesley is back to worrying about Methodism becoming a dead sect, having the form of a religion without the power. The real problem is that Methodists are becoming rich, and their devotion to God has been compromised.

There is a different diagnosis of decline that shows up shortly after his death in 1825 and may have come from his hand.

> The Methodists must take heed to their doctrine, their experience, their practice and their discipline. If they attend to their doctrines only, they will make the people antinomians; if to the experimental part of their religion, they will become Pharisees; and if they do not attend to their discipline, they will be like persons who bestow much pain in cultivating their garden, and put no fence around it, to save it from the wild boar of the forest.

However we analyse the causes of decline, Methodists have flourished outside Britain and the United States. So there will be a future.

Chapter 9
Future prospects of Methodism

Hang-glider analysis

Sorting out the future prospects of Methodism is a high-wire act. Methodism as a network of Christian churches stretches across the globe. These churches are autonomous; there is no general council or hierarchy directing developments on the ground. The most influential Methodist church—the United Methodist Church—faces the prospect of division. Looking at from above, there is a patchwork of disconnected fields whose future depends on a host of contingent factors within and without. One thing is sure. Methodism will survive. There are eighty million Christians who trace their lineage back to John Wesley. If we add to this the spiritual children and grandchildren who will join them generations later, we are looking at a quarter of a billion Christians, representing the most vibrant form of Christianity in the contemporary world.

One way to provide focal attention is to look at how Methodists tend to see their own identity and place within the history of Christianity. After all, our future actions are shaped by our identity; we become what we are. The future tense is tied in part to the present indicative. The beauty of this approach is that it allows us to review the different conceptions of Methodism that are in play. It also permits me to give my own account of what

Methodism is and of how Methodism relates to other branches of the Christian tradition.

Competing identities

I begin with a comment from Albert Outler from 1962. For Outler, Methodism was *une église manqué*:

> The drift of these comments is that Methodism has never lost the *essence* of a *functional* doctrine of the church, but that, by the same token, it has never developed—on its own and for itself—the full panoply of bell, book, and candle that goes with being a 'proper' church properly self-understood. This makes us *une église manqué* [a failed, incomplete church] theoretically and actually.

On this analysis Methodism cannot really be a network of churches; at best it can function as if it were. In the light of this observation Outler tended to see Methodism as an Evangelical Order within the Church Catholic. This Church Catholic was to be a future creation of the drive towards organic church unity. The United Methodist Church represented a first step in this direction. The follow-through would mean that the future of United Methodism lay in the integration of Methodism within a church body yet to be created. This body would emerge out of the work of the Ecumenical Movement. Churches would take the best gifts of all Christian groups and forge a new organic body with common doctrine, authority, mission, and ministry. British and Irish Methodism have been deeply committed to this agenda. Effectively, it means the end of Methodism as an independent enterprise. This has happened in Canada, India, Australia, and Sweden, where various Uniting Churches were founded. Everything hinges in this scenario on the success of efforts at church unity. In a time of new divisions this future looks bleak.

Several other options also look upon Methodism as a failed experiment in the history of Christianity. John Kent, an incisive

English historian of Methodism, has argued that Methodism is an expression of primal religion that cannot survive the shift into a full-scale church, complete with creeds, articles of religion, official ministries, general assemblies, and the like. Primary religion involves intense fears and anxieties relieved by supernatural forces; it then goes on to produce secondary theologies, breeding sects, denominations, and churches. Primary religion is not likely to disappear; but the institutional mana it produces tends to kill it. It goes stale while the primary religion re-erupts and takes off again. Some have suggested that Methodism's greatest gift to the world was to die and give rise to Pentecostalism. Clearly on this analysis there is no substantial future for Methodism, although this can be interpreted to mean a whole new lease of life for Methodism.

A more optimistic scenario is to return to the roots of Methodism and to retrieve its identity as a renewal movement within Western Christianity. The result is a raft of movements of renewal that make use of the manifold resources of Methodist churches. All remain cautiously open about the prospects of renewal within Methodism. There is no agreement on what such a renewal might look like. The Charismatic Movement continues to have impact within Methodist circles, although its influence peaked a generation ago. The Seedbed Movement is committed to working towards a Great Awakening, in which Wesleyans and Methodists would be gathered together for conferences in the United States. The New Monasticism seeks to draw on the tradition of contemplative mysticism, looking for a fresh springtime in the history of the church. Various progressive and radical networks—the 'Reconciling Congregations', 'Love Prevails'—seek to work for a more inclusive Methodism in which lesbian, gay, bisexual, transsexual, and queer (LGBTQ) Christians are given a full place in the life and ministry of the church. Liberationist networks—mostly in the academy and in the agencies of the church—hope for a political revolution above and beyond that offered by Democrats in the United States. Various evangelical and orthodox groups—the Good News Movement, the Confessing Movement, Scholars for Orthodoxy in United Methodism, and the Wesley Covenant Association—operate to uphold classical theological and moral Methodist teaching, and are in place to develop a new Methodist denomination should United Methodism divide. If these options prevail, Methodism will continue much as it is now, with various gains and losses depending on how one thinks of renewal.

A widely canvassed vision of Methodism in the United Methodist Church is to see Methodism as a mainline liberal Protestant denomination alongside the Episcopal Church, the Presbyterian Church (USA), and the Evangelical Lutheran Church. As such, Methodism can claim a full and rightful place in the church universal. On this reading, what makes Methodism different is that it houses a set of distinctive doctrines and practices, like assurance and open communion. In this scenario, United Methodism is destined to follow the recent developments in other mainline Protestant churches. It will focus on social action, rework its views on sexuality, experience decline, and then divide. Division will open the door to the formation of a new conservative and orthodox Methodist denomination that will continue globally. Such a new Methodist denomination is likely to grow in the short-term but will face all the challenges that come with division.

So these are the main options currently at play: cease to exist, being integrated into another Christian body either currently existing or yet to be invented, and if necessary accepting the doctrine and practice of apostolic succession; cease to exist as a form of primal religion and let others take up this baton in the future of religion across the world; go back behind the formation of Methodism as a network of churches and find new forms of renewal that can breathe fresh life into both Methodism and Christianity as a whole; acknowledge Methodism as a version of mainline liberal Protestant Christianity and follow the story line exhibited in sister Protestant churches; work with Methodism as a Wesleyan version of evangelicalism as contrasted with Calvinist or conservative versions of evangelicalism.

Loss of nerve

All these options fail to take a really deep look at the place of Methodism in the history of Christianity. In fact, I would go further. Donald Dayton, a polymath North American historian and theologian, has noted that in the search for identity in the 19th century, Methodists were haunted by an inferiority complex in the face of Presbyterian and Episcopal condescension. He suggests that Methodists don't know how to 'do theology'—the Presbyterian critique—or how to 'do church'—the Episcopalian critique. If Methodism is to have a future, there needs to be a recovery of nerve about its origins, its message, its practices, and its mission. Equally there needs to be a fresh way of thinking about Methodism as a full-scale church in the history of Christianity. The present prospects of fresh division open up the way for a new conversation about Methodist identity that can shape what it will become in the future.

Another look at identity

We can begin this conversation with a comment by Lesslie Newbigin, one of the outstanding church leaders of the 20th century. Newbigin divided Christianity into three streams and drew attention to a neglected third stream beyond Catholicism and Protestantism.

> Let me in a brief and preliminary way characterize this stream [that is contrasted with Catholicism and Protestantism] by saying that its central element is the conviction that the Christian life is a matter of the experienced power and pressure of the Holy Spirit today; that neither orthodoxy of doctrines nor impeccability of succession can take the place of this; that an excessive emphasis upon those immutable elements in the Gospel upon which

orthodox Catholicism and Protestantism have concentrated attention may, and in fact often does, result in a Church which is a mere shell, having the form of a Church but not the life; that if we would answer the question 'Where is the Church?,' we must ask 'Where is the Holy Spirit recognizably present with power?' Those who belong to this stream of Christian faith and life confront the orthodox Protestant and Catholic alike with words such as George Fox addressed to Margaret Fell: 'What has any to do with the Scripture, but as they came to the Spirit that gave them forth? Will you say, Christ saith this, and the apostles this; but canst thou say?'—words reminiscent of an earlier and grimmer question: 'Jesus I know and Paul I know, but who are ye?'

Newbigin does not mention Methodism, but anyone familiar with the language of 'the form of a Church but not the life' can hear characteristic Methodist leitmotifs. We can also hear a well-known theme that shows up in both academic and popular writings of Methodists—that is, 'the Holy Spirit recognizably present with power'. We are on the cusp of finding a fresh way to think of Methodism as a fully fledged church.

Three observations

Developing a fresh vision needs a short runway to take off. I will fire up its engines with three initial comments:

First, think again of Methodism as one element in the Great Awakening that spread across Europe and North America in the 18th century. Methodists saw themselves as a surprising work of God, as a movement of the Holy Spirit that was initially best described as a movement of reform and renewal. Later Methodists saw Methodism as a New Pentecost. Across the centuries this has been a recurring theme: from Phoebe Palmer in American Methodism and William Arthur in Irish Methodism in the 19th century to E. Stanley Jones (1884–1973) in American

Methodism, John Sung (1901–44) in Chinese Methodism, and Daniel T. Niles (1908–70) in Sri Lankan Methodism in the 20th century.

Second, run Methodism forward and it is easy to link it with the major movements of the Holy Spirit represented by Pentecostalism and the Charismatic movement in the 20th century. The connecting bridge is the holiness movement of the 19th century. More recently, Methodist churches in Chile, Korea, Singapore, Costa Rica, Cuba, and Africa all look like cousins of the Pentecostals (Figure 8). In Costa Rica, the Methodist Church had been reduced to about 600 members after its leaders embraced a strong version of Liberation theology. A Marxist headmaster was sent to run the Methodist High School on San Jose. When the bishop saw the writing on the wall, the whole church changed direction by going back to its Wesleyan roots and opening itself to the winds blowing through Pentecostalism. There are now over 20,000 Methodists in Costa Rica. In Cuba, the leaders prayed to God to either kill or resurrect it. The result is a church that is

8. Korean congregation.

exploding with testimonies straight out of the Acts of the Apostles. More broadly, in much of South America, many Methodist churches are in effect Pentecostal in nature without the theology and trappings of Pentecostalism. Many of the leaders in these areas have not been entirely happy with this development. They rightly note that there are no problem-free situations for the church. However, here we can see that Methodism belongs in this third stream of Christianity identified by Newbigin.

Third, run the history of Methodism backwards and we find an interesting correlation. Many Methodists have been keen to view its history from the Protestant tradition through to the Reformation in a Low Church direction or back up through the Anglican tradition into the early fathers in a High Church direction. However, there is another way to run the story that dovetails with recent efforts to elevate treasures of the monastic traditions. Wesley can be seen as mediating an ancient and continuing history that reaches right back through the early church to the New Testament. Methodism is a fresh version of primitive Christianity. In the language of David Hempton, Methodism is 'An Empire of the Spirit'.

Wesley, while he had no time for official forms of monasticism, drew heavily on elements of monastic theology and spirituality in order to understand and enrich what was happening in Methodist circles. He was influenced by Pseudo-Macarius of Egypt from the 4th century. He ransacked the writings of Spanish mystics from the 16th century. He doesn't appear to have read the works of Symeon the New Theologian from the 11th century in Greece, yet the parallels between Wesley and Symeon are remarkable. Both saw the heart of Christianity as represented in the impartation of a love for God and neighbour through the working of the Holy Spirit. Both were committed to the Lord's Supper as crucial to spiritual encounter and nourishment. Both stressed the importance of the believing in the Holy Spirit giving humble self-confidence to the believer. Both insisted on a deeper immersion in the life of the

Holy Spirit. Both rejected Augustine's views on predestination. Both challenged the idea that grace and spiritual energy necessitate the historic episcopate, the idea that grace requires that the Holy Spirit is handed down exclusively in its fullness through bishops who can trace their line back to the first apostles by the physical laying on of hands by them and their successors.

In the light of these considerations it is no surprise that Wesley did not develop a coherent doctrine of the church. He wobbled between a vision that identified the church with all the believers everywhere in the world and a vision of the church given to him as an Anglican. The latter officially taught that 'the visible Church of Christ is a congregation of faithful men in which the pure Word of God is preached, and the sacraments be duly administered'. Contrary to what Outler noted, Methodist theologians and churches in their official teachings have long wrestled with the doctrine of the church. They did so because they believed Methodism was no longer a renewal movement but a network of churches; and they did so because others asked them to do so, especially when Methodists gladly joined in efforts to secure church unity.

The two big battalions

Think of the debate initially in terms of the two big blocks of Christianity: Catholicism and Protestantism.

Consider the Catholic–Orthodox block.

Here the Church is brought into existence by bishops who stretch back in time to the apostles and who mediate spiritual realities through the ordination of priests and through the administration of the sacraments. Christian groups become a church if they are physically joined by the relevant rites of authorized priests and bishops. Thus episcopal succession—the hand-delivery of authority and grace physically through bishops—is essential to being a church. The internal debate in this block of Christians revolves around the place of the bishop of Rome in the system as a whole. Roman Catholicism insists that the bishop of Rome, as pope, has sovereignty over the whole church and possesses the grace of infallibility to secure truth in the teaching of faith and morals. Eastern Orthodox and Oriental Orthodox churches reject these claims.

Clearly Methodism does not fit this scheme, for even Wesley himself rejected the historic episcopate—the claim that there is a physical chain of continuity across time from the apostles to today's bishops—as based upon a false reading of church history.

Consider the churches stemming from the Reformation.

Let's refer to these as offering us the option of Magisterial Protestantism. Here I am thinking of the Lutheran, Presbyterian, Baptist, Reformed Anglican, Congregational, and the host of other self-professed Protestant denominations that now populate the world. In this case one hallmark of the Church is the vision of *sola scriptura* in all its variations where truth in theology, including truth about the church, is to be found by the study of scripture. Despite endless efforts that continue to this day the result is massive disagreement on the interpretation of scripture with the ensuing disagreements on the nature of ministry, mission, order, and sacraments. In the light of this, debate about the true church has sometimes been decided by state action, as happened in the case of the Church of England in 1662.

Clearly Methodism does not fit this scheme. Wesley did not believe that you could find a blueprint for order and ministry in the New Testament, even though he defended his ordinations in 1784 by appeal to his study of the New Testament. This was essentially a defensive and apologetic move; it did not tell the whole story of what a church is. The diversity of orders of ministry in Methodism across space and time bears witness to the fact that this issue is not settled by the study of the New Testament.

A third army of the Lord

Here is a third option for Methodists, given that its origins can be traced to a New Pentecost in the history of the church. Methodism should see the church normatively as the creation of the Holy Spirit brought to birth most conspicuously first time around at Pentecost and then created again and again across space and time. This work of the Holy Spirit is carried out characteristically but not exclusively through Word, sacrament, and appropriate forms of order and ministry. No-one put this better than Irenaeus, one of the great teachers and apologists of the early church in the 2nd century. 'Where the church is there is the Holy Spirit; and where the Holy Spirit is there is the church and every kind of grace.' The first half points to the fact that where we have the ministries of Word, sacrament, and ministry, then we can expect the Holy Spirit to be at work connecting the repentant hearer to the Son of God and thus forming his Body, in other words, the church. But the second half is equally important. 'Where the Holy Spirit is, there is the church and every kind of grace.' It is in this half of the aphorism that Methodism belongs; and it is the more important half for it captures the crucial agent behind the creation of the church, namely the good and life-giving Holy Spirit. This is not a full-scale doctrine of the church, but it is a good start. Adopting and developing this vision of itself as church gives no guarantee of a bright future for Methodists but I think it will be essential to a bright future.

This way of thinking about the church requires fresh thinking about the history of the church. Catholicism and Protestantism think of the church in a linear way. They both read the history of the church as one of uni-directional development across time. For Roman Catholicism this is a story of complex changes from the apostles till today. For Protestants the story is one of broken development. Hence the basic options for Protestants are basically twofold. Reform the church and fix the parts of it that represent illegitimate developments, as we find argued by Luther and

Calvin. Or, more radically, restore the ancient church once and for all, as we find, say, among the Plymouth Brethren or the Churches of Christ in the United States.

Consider, however, a very different way of thinking of the relation between the current expression of the church and her history. Think of the church not in terms of linear development but in terms of an original prototype and its fresh expression or reproduction across space and time. The crucial agent in the creation of the church is the Triune God. Suppose God has a prototype for the church. Then the church can be created across space and time by God from the top down by the outpouring of the Holy Spirit. The Spirit provides the church with all the resources it needs—scripture, ministries, sacraments, creeds, oversight, councils, and so on—and thus a group which begins as a renewal movement can, like the first Christians, become a true church. As an initial renewal movement within Judaism the early church did not need to have physical succession, for Paul rejected the notion and the practice. Nor did it need to have a New Testament, for the first Christians did not have the expanded Bible we now possess. Where the Spirit is, there is the church. Methodists have to hand a vision of its churches as creations of the Holy Spirit, the third person of the Trinity who provides it with all that it needs to be a church and to carry out Christ's mission today. Within this there is a place for various kinds of groups which keep alive the fire of renewal (Figure 9).

I am suggesting here that it is a mistake to think that one can turn the clock back and think of Methodism as a renewal movement. One can gain solace and inspiration in doing this but history has moved on. Nor can one think of Methodism as one more edition of mainline liberal Protestantism with its own distinctive doctrines and practices. This looks illuminating if one lives in the United States but it is a parochial vision that is undermined by reality. United Methodism is not one more mainline Protestant denomination; it is a unique, global expression of

9. **Women's Manyano.**

ancient Christianity. The critical mistake is to think merely in terms of sociological observations about identity. The crucial observation to make is this: one and only one body both represents and speaks for the United Methodist Church, namely, the General Conference. Anecdotal remarks about a local church, or seminary faculties, or national data, or even the Council of Bishops are beside the point. It is the General Conference and only the General Conference that speaks for the United Methodist Church as a whole. In this respect the United Methodist Church is ineradicably conciliar in nature. Moreover, the delegates to the General Conference are elected in terms of demographic allocation. They are literally the representatives, lay and clergy, of the church as whole.

A lasting work of God

John Wesley once noted that what God had achieved in the development of Methodism was no mere human endeavour but the work of God.

> We have strong reason to hope that the work [God] hath begun he will carry on unto the day of the Lord Jesus; that he will never intermit this blessed work of the Spirit until he has fulfilled his

119

promises; until he hath put a period to sin and misery, and infirmity, and death; and re-established universal holiness and happiness, and caused all the inhabitants of the earth to sing together, 'Hallelujah! The Lord God omnipotent reigneth!' 'Blessing and glory, and wisdom, and honour, and power, and might be unto our God for ever and ever!'

So Methodism would be preserved by God so long as history remains. The place for the continued preservation of the treasures given to Methodism by God belongs in a new configuration of Methodism. Some wistfully but rightfully envisage a new global, orthodox Methodist denomination that would begin from within United Methodism and then over the next decades expand by adding other Wesleyan and Methodist bodies across the world. Strong Methodist denominations that are flourishing and smaller Methodist denominations that are currently struggling could find a bigger home in which to grow and flourish. All this would take time, determined persistence, and wise leadership; but these are available in spades. The goal would be to preserve a robust orthodox and missionary version of United Methodism. It is an open question how exactly this might be done. The relationships, mechanisms, and personnel are in place to determine joint action as and where it would be needed. For the moment we are in a period of unsettled incubation. In the long-term the prospects and outcomes lie in the providence of God. It would be bold but not impossible to believe that providence might include another Great Awakening in its portfolio.

The Roots, Classical Development, and Offshoots of Methodism

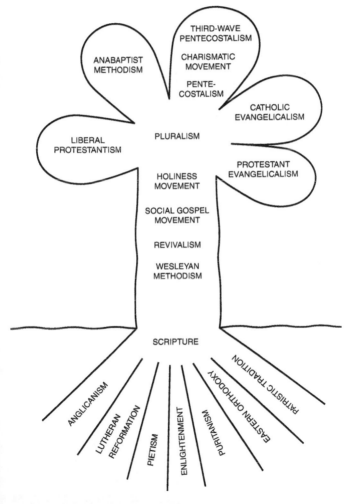

References

Chapter 1: John Wesley and the origins of Methodism

'In the evening I went very unwillingly…' John Wesley, *The Works of John Wesley*, Volume 18: *Journals and Diaries, I (1735–38)*, ed. W. Reginald Ward and Richard P. Heitzenrater (Nashville: Abingdon Press, 1988), 249–50.

'"Do you hope to be saved?" [asked Böhler]…' Charles Wesley, *The Journal of the Rev. Charles Wesley M.A., Sometime Student of Christ Church, Oxford, the Early Journal, 1736–1739* (Taylors: Methodist Reprint Society, 1977), 134–5.

'At eight I prayed for myself…' Charles Wesley, *The Journal of the Rev. Charles Wesley M.A., Sometime Student of Christ Church, Oxford, the Early Journal, 1736–1739* (Taylors: Methodist Reprint Society, 1977), 153.

'At four in the afternoon…' John Wesley, *The Works of John Wesley*, Volume 19: *Journals and Diaries, I (1738–43)*, ed. W. Reginald Ward and Richard P. Heitzenrater (Nashville: Abingdon Press, 1990), 46.

'The House was filled at five…' John Wesley, *The Works of John Wesley*, Volume 23: *Journals and Diaries, I (1776–86)*, ed. W. Reginald Ward and Richard P. Heitzenrater (Nashville: Abingdon Press, 1995), 141–2.

'Suffer me now to tell you…' John Wesley, *The Works of John Wesley*, Volume 19: *Journals and Diaries, I (1738–43)*, ed. W. Reginald Ward and Richard P. Heitzenrater (Nashville: Abingdon Press, 1990), 67.

'Can you bear the summer heat…' John Wesley, *The Works of John Wesley*, Volume 11: *The Appeals to Men of Reason and Religion and Certain Related Open Letters*, ed. Gerald R. Cragg (Nashville: Abingdon Press, 1989), 307.

'Today I learned for the first time…' The description by the visiting scholar from Uppsala is taken from Richard Heitzenrater, *The Elusive Mr Wesley* (Nashville: Abingdon, 1984), 2: 87–8.

Chapter 2: Supporting background stimuli

'to reform England…' Thomas Jackson (ed.), *The Works of the Rev. John Wesley, M.A.*, 14 vols. (London: Mason, 1829–31; reprinted by Grand Rapids: Baker Book House, 1978), 299.

'Let us observe what God…' John Wesley, *The Works of John Wesley*, Volume 2: *Sermons II 34–70* (Nashville: Abingdon Press, 1985), edited by Albert Outler, 490–1.

'When the question of the validity…' E. Stanley Jones, *The Christ of Every Road, A Study in Pentecost* (New York: Abingdon Press, 1930), 111.

Chapter 7: The impact of Methodism

'Yet even with such attitudes…' Kenneth Cracknell and Susan J. White, *An Introduction to World Methodism* (Cambridge: Cambridge University Press, 2005), 90.

'The professorial lectures are useless…' Henry D. Rack, *Reasonable Enthusiast, John Wesley and the Rise of Methodism* (Philadelphia: Trinity Press International, 1989), 357.

Chapter 8: The decline of Methodism

'Observe: It is not your business…' Rule 11 of John Wesley's 'Twelve Rules for Preachers'.

'I am not afraid that the people…' John Wesley, 'Thoughts upon Methodism,' in Rupert P. Davis (ed.), *The Works of John Wesley*, Volume 9: *The Methodist Societies, History, Nature, and Design* (Nashville: Abingdon, 1989), 527.

'…the church is dying a slow death…' Stanley Hauerwas and William H. Willimon, *Resident Aliens* (Nashville: Abingdon Press, 1989), 167.

'Does this not seem (and yet…)' John Wesley, *The Works of John Wesley*, Volume 4: *Sermons IV 115–51*, ed. Albert Outler (Nashville: Abingdon Press, 1987), 95–6.

'The Methodists must take heed…' Attributed to one of Wesley's preachers in reference to a question put to Wesley in 1783. However, the exact source is unknown.

Chapter 9: Future prospects of Methodism

'The drift of these comments is…' Albert Cook Outler, 'Do Methodists Have a Doctrine of the Church?', in Thomas C. Oden and Leicester R. Longden (eds.), *The Wesleyan Theological Heritage, Essays of Albert C. Outler* (Grand Rapids: Zondervan, 1991), 224.

'Let me in a brief and preliminary way…' Lesslie Newbigin, *The Household of God* (New York: Friendship Press, 1954), 95.

'the visible Church of Christ…' John Wesley, *The Works of John Wesley*, Volume 2: *Sermons II 34–70*, ed. Albert Outler (Nashville: Abingdon Press, 1985), 499.

'Where the church is there…' Irenaeus, *Adv. Haer.* 3.24.1.

'We have strong reason to hope…' John Wesley, *The Works of John Wesley*, Volume 2: *Sermons II 34–70*, ed. Albert Outler (Nashville: Abingdon Press, 1985), 499.

Further reading

General

William J. Abraham and James E. Kirby (eds.), *The Oxford Handbook of Methodist Studies* (Oxford: Oxford University Press, 2009).

Frank Baker (ed.), *The Bicentennial Edition of the Works of John Wesley* (Nashville: Abingdon Press, 1975–).

Ted A. Campbell, *Encoding Methodism: Telling and Retelling Narratives of Wesleyan Origins* (Nashville: New Room Books, 2017).

Kenneth Cracknell, and Susan J. White, *An Introduction to World Methodism* (Cambridge: Cambridge University Press, 2005).

William Gibson, Peter Forsaith, and Martin Wellings (eds.), *The Ashgate Research Companion to World Methodism* (Burlington: Ashgate, 2013).

Richard P. Heitzenrater, *Mirror and Memory: Reflections on Early Methodism* (Nashville: Abingdon Press, 1989).

David Hempton, *Methodism, Empire of the Spirit* (New Haven: Yale University Press, 2005).

John Kent, *Wesley and the Wesleyans, Religion in Eighteenth Century Great Britain* (Cambridge: Cambridge University Press, 2002).

Randy L. Maddox and Jason E. Vickers (eds.), *The Cambridge Companion to John Wesley* (Cambridge: Cambridge University Press, 2010).

J. Steven O'Malley and Jason E. Vickers (eds.), *Methodist and Pietist: Retrieving the Evangelical United Brethren Tradition* (Nashville: Kingswood Books, 2011).

Albert C. Outler, *John Wesley, a Representative Collection of his Writings* (New York: Oxford University Press, 1964).

Russell E. Richey, Kenneth E. Rowe, and Jean Miller Schmidt (eds.), *Perspectives on American Methodism: Interpretive Essays* (Nashville: Kingswood Books, 1993).

Norman W. Taggart, *The Irish in World Methodism 1760–1900* (London: Epworth Press, 1986).

Jason E. Vickers (ed.), *The Cambridge Companion to American Methodism* (New York: Cambridge University Press, 2013).

W. Reginald Ward, *Early Evangelicalism: A Global Intellectual History 1670–1789* (Cambridge: Cambridge University Press, 2006).

Charles Yrigoven (ed.), *T&T Clark Companion to Methodism* (London and New York: T&T Clark, 2014).

Chapter 1: John Wesley and the origins of Methodism

J. C. D. Clark, *English Society 1650–1832* (Cambridge: Cambridge University Press, 2002).

Ryan Nicholas Danker, *Wesley and the Anglicans, Political Division in Early Evangelicalism* (Downers Grove: IVP Academic, 2016).

Donald W. Dayton, 'Methodism and Pentecostalism', in William J. Abraham and James E. Kirby (eds.), *The Oxford Handbook of Methodist Studies* (Oxford: Oxford University Press, 2009), 171–87.

Richard P. Heitzenrater, *The Elusive Mr Wesley* (Nashville: Abingdon Press, 1984), 2 vols.

Kenneth G. C. Newport and Ted A. Campbell (eds.), *Charles Wesley: Life, Literature and Legacy* (Peterborough: Epworth, 2007).

Robert Southey, *The Life of John Wesley, and the Rise and Progress of Methodism* (London: Frederick Warne and Co., 1889).

Jason E. Vickers, *John Wesley, a Guide for the Perplexed* (London: T&T Clark, 2009).

Rowan Williams, 'John Wesley, a Fool for Christ, a Sermon Preached at Christ Church, Oxford', *Fairacres Chronicle* 21 (1988), 8–12.

Chapter 2: Supporting background stimuli

James T. Campbell, *Songs of Zion: The African-American Episcopal Church in the United States and South Africa* (New York: Oxford University Press, 1995).

Justo L. Gonzalez (ed.), *Each in Our Own Tongue: A History of Hispanics in United Methodism* (Nashville: Abingdon Press, 1991).

Richard Heitzenrater, *Wesley and the People Called Methodists* (Nashville: Abingdon Press, 1995).

William B. McClain, 'African American Methodists: A Remnant and a Reminder', in Russell Richey, Dennis M. Campbell, and William B. Lawrence (eds.), *United Methodism and American Culture*, Volume 1: *Connectionalism: Ecclesiology, Mission, and Identity* (Nashville: Abingdon Press, 1997), 77–94.

Henry Rack, *Reasonable Enthusiast, John Wesley and the Rise of Methodism* (Philadelphia: Trinity Press International, 1989).

Patrick Philip Streiff, *Methodism in Europe: 19th and 20th Century* (Tallinn: Baltic Methodist Theological Seminary, 2003).

Philip Wingeier-Rayo, *Cuban Methodism: The Untold Story of Revival and Survival* (Lawrenceville: Dolphins & Orchids Pub., 2004).

Charles Yrigoyen, Jr (ed.), *The Global Impact of Wesleyan Traditions and their Related Movements* (London: The Scarecrow Press, Inc., 2002).

Chapter 3: The people called Methodists

Robert E. Chiles, *Theological Transition in American Methodism, 1790–1935* (New York: University Press of America, 1983).

Kenneth J. Collins, *The Theology of John Wesley, Holy Love and the Shape of Grace* (Nashville: Abingdon, 2007).

Kenneth J. Collins and Jason E. Vickers (ed.), *The Sermons of John Wesley, a Collection for the Christian Journey* (Nashville: Abingdon Press, 2013).

Kenneth Cracknell, *Our Doctrines, Methodist Theology and Classical Christianity* (Calver: Cliff College Publishing, 1998).

Elden Dale Dunlap, 'Methodist Theology in Great Britain in the Nineteenth Century', Yale University Ph.D. thesis, 1956.

Scott J. Jones, *United Methodist Doctrine, the Extreme Center* (Nashville: Abingdon Press, 2002).

Randy L. Maddox, *Responsible Grace: John Wesley's Practical Theology* (Nashville: Kingswood Books, 1994).

Thomas C. Oden, *John Wesley's Scriptural Christianity: A Plain Exposition of his Teaching on Christian Doctrine* (Grand Rapids: Zondervan, 1994).

Thomas C. Oden and Leicester C. Longden (eds.), *The Wesleyan Theological Heritage, Essays of Albert C. Outler* (Grand Rapids: Zondervan, 1991).

Albert C. Outler, *Theology in the Wesleyan Spirit* (Nashville: Tidings, 1975).

Albert C. Outler and Richard P. Heitzenrater (eds.), *John Wesley's Sermons: An Anthology* (Nashville: Abingdon Press, 1991).

J. Ernest Rattenbury, *The Evangelical Doctrines of Charles Wesley's Hymns* (London: Epworth Press, 1941).

John Wesley, *Sermons on Several Occasions* (London: Epworth Press, 1944).

Kenneth Wilson, *Methodist Theology* (London: T&T Clark, 2011)

Chapter 4: The message of Methodism

Ole Edvard Borgen, *John Wesley and the Sacraments: A Theological Study* (Nashville: Abingdon Press, 1972).

Gale Carlton Felton, *The Gift of Water: The Practice and Theology of Baptism Among Methodists in America* (Nashville: Abingdon Press, 1992).

James E. Kirby, *The Episcopacy in American Methodism* (Nashville: Kingswood Books, 2000).

Henry H. Knight III, *The Presence of God in the Christian Life: John Wesley and the Means of Grace* (Metuchen: Scarecrow Press, 1992).

Henry H. Knight III, *Eight Life-Enriching Practices of United Methodists* (Nashville: Abingdon Press, 2001).

J. Ernest Rattenbury, *The Eucharistic Hymns of John and Charles Wesley* (London: Epworth Press, 1948).

Russell E. Richey, *The Methodist Conference in America* (Nashville: Kingswood Books, 1996).

Mark Wesley Stamm, *Sacraments and Discipleship: Understanding Baptism and the Lord's Supper in a United Methodist Context* (Ashland City: OSL Publications, 2013).

David Lowes Watson, *The Early Methodist Class Meeting: Its Origins and Significance* (Nashville: Abingdon Press, 1985).

David Lowes Watson, *Covenant Discipleship: Christian Formation through Mutual Accountability* (Nashville: Discipleship Resources, 1991).

Kevin M. Watson, *Pursuing Social Holiness: The Band Meeting in Wesley's Thought and Popular Methodist Practice* (New York: Oxford University Press, 2014).

Kevin M. Watson, *The Class Meeting: Reclaiming a Forgotten (and Essential) Small Group Experience* (Wilmore: Seedbed Publishing, 2014).

Chapter 5: The search for credible alternatives

Henry Abelove, *The Evangelist of Desire: John Wesley and the Methodists* (Stanford: Stanford University Press, 1990).

Nathan O. Hatch, *The Democratization of American Culture* (New Haven: Yale University Press, 1989).

Nathan O. Hatch and John H. Wigger (eds.), *Methodism and the Shaping of American Culture* (Nashville: Kingswood Books, 2001).

David Hempton, *Methodism and Politics in British Society, 1750–1850* (London: Hutchinson, 1984).

Elmer Brooks Holifield, *Health and Medicine in the Methodist Tradition* (New York: Crossroad, 1986).

Nigel Scotland, 'Methodism and the English Labor Movement 1800–1906', *Anvil* 14 (1997), 36–48.

Bernard Semmel, *The Methodist Revolution* (London: Heinemann, 1974).

Edward P. Thompson, *The Making of the English Working Class* (London: Gollancz, 1963).

W. Reginald Ward, *Religion and Society 1790–1850* (London: Batsford, 1972).

Elliott Wright, 'American Methodism and Public Education: 1784 to 1900', in Dennis M. Campbell, William B. Lawrence, and Russell E. Richey (eds.), *United Methodism and American Culture, Volume 3: Doctrines and Discipline* (Nashville: Abingdon Press, 1999), 181–98.

Chapter 6: The practices of Methodism

Steve Bruce, *God is Dead: Secularization in the West* (Oxford: Blackwell, 2002).

Ted A. Campbell, *The Sky is Falling, the Church is Dying, and other False Alarms* (Nashville: Abingdon Press, 2015).

Stanley Hauerwas and William H. Willimon, *Resident Aliens, A Provocative Christian Assessment of Culture and Ministry for People Who Know that Something Is Wrong* (Nashville: Abingdon Press, 1989).

Elaine A. Heath and Scott T. Kisker, *Longing for Spring: A New Vision for Wesleyan Community* (Eugene: Cascade Books, 2010).

George Hunter III, *To Spread the Power, Church Growth in the Wesleyan Spirit* (Nashville: Abingdon Press, 1987).

Joerg Rieger and John Vincent (eds.), *Methodist and Radical: Rejuvenating a Tradition* (Nashville: Kingswood Books, 2003).

Richard B. Wilkie, *And Are We Yet Alive? The Future of the United Methodist Church* (Nashville: Abingdon Press, 1986).

Philip J. Wogaman, *To Serve the Present Age: The Gift and Promise of Methodism* (Nashville: Abingdon Press, 1995).

Linda Woodhead and Rebecca Catto (eds.), *Religion and Change in Modern Britain* (London: Routledge, 2012).

Chapter 7: The impact of Methodism

William J. Abraham, *Celtic Fire: Evangelism in the Wisdom and Power of the Spirit* (Dallas: Highland Loch Press, 2012).

William J. Abraham, 'The Place of Methodism in the History of Christianity', *Bulletin of the Irish Methodist Historical Society of Ireland* 21 (2016), 5–19.

William Arthur, *The Tongue of Fire; or the True Power of Christianity* (Nashville: Publishing House of the M. E. Church, South, 1920).

Elaine A. Heath, *Naked Faith, the Mystical Theology of Phoebe Palmer* (Eugene: Pickwick Publications, 2009).

Lim Ka-Tong, *The Life and Ministry of John Sung* (Singapore: Genesis Books, 2012).

Paul M. Minus (ed.), *Methodist Destiny in an Ecumenical Age* (Nashville: Abingdon Press, 1969).

Lesslie Newbigin, *The Household of God, Lectures on the Nature of the Church* (New York: Friendship Press, 1954).

Thomas C. Oden, *The Rebirth of Orthodoxy, Signs of New Life in Christianity* (San Francisco: Harper, 2003).

Albert C. Outler, 'Do Methodists Have a Doctrine of the Church?', in Dow Kirkpatrick (ed.), *The Doctrine of the Church* (Nashville: Abingdon Press, 1964), 11–28.

Russell E. Richey, William B. Lawrence, and Dennis M. Campbell (eds.), *United Methodism and American Culture*, Volume 4: *Questions for the Twenty-First Century Church* (Nashville: Abingdon Press, 1999).

Edgar W. Thompson, *The Methodist Doctrine of the Church* (London: Epworth Press, 1939).

Publisher's acknowledgements

We are grateful for permission to include the following copyright material in this book.

Extract from Luckenbach, Texas
Words & Music by Chips Moman & Bobby Emmons.
© Copyright 1980 Baby Chick Music.
Universal Music Publishing Limited.
All Rights Reserved. International Copyright Secured.
Used by Permission of Hal Leonard Europe Limited.

The publisher and author have made every effort to trace and contact all copyright holders before publication. If notified, the publisher will be pleased to rectify any errors or omissions at the earliest opportunity.

Index

Methodism

Index

SOCIAL MEDIA
Very Short Introduction

Join our community
www.oup.com/vsi

- Join us online at the official Very Short Introductions **Facebook** page.
- Access the thoughts and musings of our authors with our online **blog**.
- Sign up for our monthly **e-newsletter** to receive information on all new titles publishing that month.
- Browse the full range of Very Short Introductions online.
- Read **extracts** from the Introductions for free.
- If you are a teacher or lecturer you can order inspection copies quickly and simply via our website.

BIBLICAL ARCHAEOLOGY
A Very Short Introduction
Eric H. Cline

Archaeologist Eric H. Cline here offers a complete overview of this exciting field. He discusses the early pioneers, the origins of biblical archaeology as a discipline, and the major controversies that first prompted explorers to go in search of sites that would "prove" the Bible. He then surveys some of the most well-known modern archaeologists, the sites that are essential sources of knowledge for biblical archaeology, and some of the most important discoveries that have been made in the last half century, including the Dead Sea Scrolls and the Tel Dan Stele.

CATHOLICISM
A Very Short Introduction
Gerald O'Collins

Despite a long history of external threats and internal strife, the
Roman Catholic Church and the broader reality of Catholicism
remain a vast and valuable presence into the third millennium of
world history. What are the origins of the Catholic Church? How
has Catholicism changed and adapted to such vast and diverse
cultural influences over the centuries? What great challenges
does the Catholic Church now face in the twenty-first century,
both within its own life and in its relation to others around the
world? In this Very Short Introduction, Gerald O'Collins draws on
the best current scholarship available to answer these questions
and to present, in clear and accessible language, a fresh
introduction to the largest and oldest institution in the world.

CHRISTIAN ETHICS
A Very Short Introduction
D. Stephen Long

This *Very Short Introduction* to Christian ethics introduces the topic by examining its sources and historical basis. D. Stephen Long presents a discussion of the relationship between Christian ethics, modern, and postmodern ethics, and explores practical issues including sex, money, and power. Long recognises the inherent difficulties in bringing together 'Christian' and 'ethics' but argues that this is an important task for both the Christian faith and for ethics. Arguing that Christian ethics are not a precise science, but the cultivation of practical wisdom from a range of sources, Long also discusses some of the failures of the Christian tradition, including the crusades, the conquest, slavery, inquisitions, and the Galileo affair.

www.oup.com/vsi

FUNDAMENTALISM
A Very Short Introduction
Malise Ruthven

Malise Ruthven tackles the polemic and stereotypes surrounding this complex phenomenon - one that eludes him today, a conclusion impossible to ignore since the events in New York on September 11 2001. But what does 'fundamentalism' really mean? Since it was coined by American Protestant evangelicals in the 1920s, the use of the term 'fundamentalist' has expanded to include a diverse range of radical conservatives and ideological purists, not all religious. Ruthven investigates fundamentalism's historical, social, religious, political, and ideological roots, and tackles the polemic and stereotypes surrounding this complex phenomenon - one that eludes simple definition, yet urgently needs to be understood.

'...powerful stuff...this book is perceptive and important.'

Observer

Mormonism
A Very Short Introduction
Richard Lyman Bushman

Mormonism is frequently described as the most successful
indigenous American religion. Mormon beliefs arouse curiosity
because they depart from normal Christian doctrine, leading
to the question: Are Mormons Christian? This introduction
will include the history of the contemporary Mormonism,
and an analysis and emphasis of Mormon beliefs, beginning
with Joseph Smith, the founding prophet.

www.oup.com/vsi

RELIGION IN AMERICA
A Very Short Introduction
Timothy Beal

Timothy Beal describes many aspects of religion in contemporary America that are typically ignored in other books on the subject, including religion in popular culture and counter-cultural groups; the growing phenomenon of "hybrid" religious identities, both individual and collective; the expanding numbers of new religious movements, or NRMs, in America; and interesting examples of "outsider religion." He also offers an engaging overview of the history of religion in America, from Native American traditions to the present day. Finally, Beal highlights the three major forces shaping the present and future of religion in America.

www.oup.com/vsi